The Green Light of Forgiveness
A Meditation on Forgiveness to take Total Control over Your Life after Trauma

Toshia Shaw

Published by Purple Wings Publishing
Copyright ©2016 by Toshia Shaw

All rights reserved, without limiting the rights under copyright reserved above. No part of this book may be reproduced, stored in or introduced into a retrieval system, or transmitted, in any form, or by any means (electronic, mechanical, photocopying, recording, or otherwise), without prior written consent from both the author, and publisher, Purple Wings Publishing, except brief quotes used in reviews.

ISBN 978-0974042664

I have tried to recreate events, locales, and conversations from my memories of them. In order to maintain their anonymity in some instances, I have changed the names of individuals and places; I may have changed some identifying characteristics and details such as physical properties, occupations, and places of residence. This book is not intended as a substitute for the medical advice of physicians or clinical therapists. The reader should regularly consult a physician or clinical therapist in matters relating to his/her health and particularly with respect to any symptoms that may require diagnosis or medical attention.

Cover Copyright © 2016 by Purple Wings Publishing.
All rights reserved

Purple Wings Publishing
3180 W. Sahara Ave.,
Ste C-20
Las Vegas, Nevada 89102

To Tristan, and Trinity thank you for being my driving force and the reason for it all…

Table of Contents

Introduction 1
1. Trauma 4
2. Practitioners....................................16
3. Healing Practices..........................26
4. Energy Healing..............................48
5. The Pain of Remembering...........58
6. Anger is a False Friend................66
7. Breathe through it........................70
8. Affirmations & Mantras................76
9. You want me to do what?............80
10. Exactly what is Forgiveness? 84
11. When it's Too Late 90
12. The Green Light of Forgiveness Meditation........94
13. Cut the Cord!..............................106
14. Boundaries..................................112
15. Release Shame & Guilt..............118
16. Divine Connection.....................124
17. Rebuild with Positive Thinking..........130
18. The Pact......................................136
19. Conclusion.................................143
20. About the author
21. References

> *"Forgiveness is not an occasional act, it is a constant attitude."*
>
> ~ Martin Luther King Jr.

Introduction

To forgive those who have caused you pain can feel as if you are giving them a free pass to walk all over you as though you're a doormat. It can feel as if you are giving the person, or the situation total control while leaving you helpless and vulnerable. I am here to tell you this is not the case at all. To forgive someone that caused you pain, turmoil, or trauma is actually an act of bravery.

It's the one thing that can heal you, and give you total freedom in your mind, body, and soul. When I approached the idea of actually forgiving the people in my life, who caused me trauma, I was apprehensive and actually defiant. I thought to myself, "Why in the world would I, could I, forgive those who purposely put my life in danger, or stomped all over me as if I meant nothing?" Then, a wave of peace came over me, and instinctively I knew that if I didn't forgive them, I would not be able to peacefully move forward.

I knew I would be bound, immobilized, and stuck in that space of hurt caused by the pain of trauma, for the rest of my life. I was tired of dwelling on a low vibration; being angry, tired of pointing fingers, and tired of holding that space that seemed to swell within my stomach every day. I suffered physically from allowing anger to consume me. I suffered from stomach ulcers, headaches, high blood pressure, and terrible panic attacks. I knew it was all due to the stress generated from being angry.

After I survived the horrific trauma of being sex-trafficked in my twenties, I suffered from post-traumatic stress disorder (PTSD). I knew something had to change. I knew I had to take back my life and let go of everything that did not bring me peace and happiness. I had to finally just forgive. I needed to forgive myself first before I could forgive anyone else—it was no easy task. In fact, it was easier to forgive others before I could forgive myself.

I want you to know that the act of forgiving is a daily task. I have to forgive someone or myself every day. It could be something as trivial as reacting to the person who cut me off in traffic, the person behind the counter who sneered at me in such a bad customer relation, or myself for not treating my body correctly because of the food I ate. Therefore, forgiveness is ongoing and should be practiced as much as possible.

I speak of God a great deal in this book; I refer to God as a *He*. I also use the names *Creator* and *The Divine* interchangeably. Simply put, God is; it doesn't matter if you call God a male or female because God is both. God just is. God is the head of my life, and Jesus Christ is my comforter. If you are not a believer, then it may be hard for you to believe there is an Entity greater than all of us—an entity that is above us all, and a Spirit that dwells in us. However, it will be hard to deny this truth once you begin to practice forgiveness and finally connect with the Divine.

You will feel that Entity slowly creep in, take up space, and transform your life. The *Green Light of Forgiveness* meditation that I created has transformed lives. It singularly transformed mine. The *Green Light of Forgiveness* meditation is used as alternative healing. This energy work is necessary as a way to complete and internal healing; as it is a complement to other forms of traditional medicine should you choose to go that route.

With the application of this alternative healing, many people have been able to forgive transgressions or shortcomings of others, such as cheating spouses, neglectful parents, chronic liars within families, and even worst of all, those who committed *seemingly* unforgiveable crimes like sexual molestation, rape, violent crimes, and even murder.

Trust me, forgiving is not easy, and people who have not evolved emotionally can't even fathom forgiving someone who caused so much pain. It can also have others questioning your sanity. I have been called crazy for forgiving others.

Ever since I've forgiven the people that caused much of my trauma, I have been the happiest, even more than I have ever been since childhood. In fact, I have gone on to new heights, vibrated higher, and achieved more success than I ever thought possible. This came to be all because I practiced forgiveness, which is the first step in being compassionate towards self and others.

It is my hope that you will utilize this book to learn what forgiveness truly is, and apply the *Green Light of Forgiveness* to those areas in your life that are holding you hostage, thereby disallowing you to heal, and move forward. Open your heart, your mind, and get ready to be blessed; and most of all, get ready to heal.

In Love & Light,

Toshia
SHAW

Chapter 1
Trauma

"PTSD is a difficult challenge that requires strong faith in order to meet that challenge and win."

Let's get definitions and scientific mumbo jumbo out of the way first so that we can dive into the juicy stuff. Just what is *trauma*? Trauma is described as an experience that causes upheaval in your typical, day-to-day routine; it's an intensely upsetting or disturbing emotional response to a heartbreaking event. When we talk about trauma, we are usually speaking of experiences that are outside of normal human occurrences, moments that felt as if you were in a dream when they took place. It's important to note that some people live with trauma on a daily basis; it becomes their "new normal," and they adapt to their traumatic environment. An example of this is people who live in a war-torn country—the people of Syria, for example. They have suffered unimaginable tragedies with death being the backdrop of their lives on a nearly daily basis. If we look at what's going on in our own country, we can see that people who live in America's most violent neighborhoods and confront gun violence on a constant basis are suffering from trauma as well.

When I first formed Purple W.I.N.G.S. Organization (PWs), my non-profit mentoring agency for at-risk girls in Las Vegas, Nevada, I ran it out of a community center in an area called West Las Vegas. This area was coined, the urban or bad part of Vegas. Being from Memphis, Tennessee and growing up partially in some tough neighborhoods, I knew what the bad parts of a city entailed. Therefore, it came as no shock when some of my younger participants as young as eight years old would tell me eye-witness tales of violent murders, homelessness, drug addicted parents, sexual assaults, and physical violence. One set of young 8-year old twins got a kick out of me when I scolded them about being outside past 7 o'clock. They were used to staying outside until 10 or sometimes 11 at night. Their parents had left them with their aunt, and they once witnessed a murder right there in their apartment complex. I think it's pretty safe to say that these young ladies experienced traumatic events on a regular basis, but had grown accustomed to them. Traumatic events include, but are not limited to, the following:

- Natural disasters
- Accidents
- Death
- Violence and assault
- Military combat/war
- Terrorism incidents
- Neglect
- Bullying

Post-Traumatic Stress Disorder, or PTSD as it is commonly referred to, is a psychiatric disorder that can occur following the experience or witnessing of any of the above or any other traumatic event. After someone suffers from a traumatic experience, it's normal for that person to be in shock and experience emotions such as being upset, sad, anxious, panicked, and disconnected. However, when someone can't quite get past those feelings, when they feel trapped by them, and their regular actions and behaviors are impaired, they may be experiencing PTSD. PTSD is a leading cause of chronic disease in North America.

Signs and Symptoms

PTSD can take hours, days, weeks, and even years to develop and appear. Some symptoms include, but are not limited to, the following: [1]

- Difficulty in mental concentration
- Feeling jumpy, easily startled
- Difficulty in falling or staying asleep
- Irritability or outbursts of anger
- Hyper-vigilance (on constant "red alert")

Often when the onset is delayed, a person might not even know that it is PTSD. When symptoms take six months or later to occur following a traumatizing event, it's called delayed onset PTSD.

Veronica came to see me because she was having a hard time. She was unable to eat, sleep, or do things as she normally had. She stated that it just happened all of a sudden. The symptoms were so bad she was having suicidal ideation. I asked her if something traumatic happened to her recently, and she said that nothing unusual happened to her and that she just started to feel this way out of the blue. Upon further questioning, I found out that she was involved in a major car accident five years earlier, wherein she was on the passenger side, and her friend was driving. A woman ran a red light, hit them, and her friend was hospitalized for almost six months. There were times they didn't think the friend would make it. Veronica vehemently denied that the accident was the reason she was experiencing insomnia, anxiety, or unable to drive on the highway. That's right, she admitted that she hated driving on the highway after further questioning. Bingo! The symptoms were there all along. Along with her not liking to drive on the highway, she had anxiety regarding driving, and didn't like driving at night.

Delayed onset PTSD is very real, and the symptoms usually show earlier but the suffering person is largely unable to pinpoint or recognize them. In Veronica's situation after talking with her extensively about the past accident, we concluded that she most definitely was having PTSD from the ordeal and never properly received the closure or healing needed to get past the accident.

Other common symptoms of post-traumatic stress disorder (PTSD):

- Guilt, shame, or self-blame
- Substance abuse
- Feelings of mistrust and betrayal
- Depression and hopelessness
- Suicidal thoughts and feelings
- Physical aches and pains

Triggers

After experiencing or witnessing trauma and developing PTSD symptoms, practically, anything can provoke emotions and memories, seemingly out of the blue. I can remember doing something as simple as listening to music and a certain song could come on the radio and flood my memory. At that moment, the song became a trigger. Some things that can trigger emotions and memories are:

- Certain sounds (like the sound of someone's voice), music, sights, or smells
- Dreams and nightmares
- Seeing or reading the news
- Seeing a person related to the event
- The anniversary date of the event

My father is a Vietnam veteran who suffers from PTSD. Every 4th of July, we have to remind our neighbors that he has PTSD, and fireworks can trigger his memory of fighting in the war, their thoughtfulness as well as sympathy during their celebratory events is greatly appreciated.

Another example comes from a woman who visited me at my office to ask if I would speak at her event. She was a retired police officer who became heavily involved with women's rights and anti-trafficking work. She sat in front of me and looked me into my eyes, and asked me for the name of my trafficker. I was caught off-guard by her question, and it became a trigger for me. Remembering my boundaries, I politely declined to answer, and told her that it was an inappropriate question. I also told that she should be mindful whenever she speaks with survivors, to avoid triggering their emotions with questions that may be deemed as insensitive. I held no ill feeling toward her because I was sure she had no idea that her question was a trigger, or deemed insensitive.

Why is there Trauma Anyway?

It's hard to understand why God would allow trauma to happen at all. But God is love, and trauma is not. Therefore, we shouldn't associate trauma with God, because He did not create it. Can He prevent it? Yes, He can but, most times, He will not interfere with the events taking place in our earthly sphere. Trust me, this was difficult for me to internalize and understand because for a long time I was angry with God for the trauma I experienced in my life. I felt that God didn't like me, and that He was just idly standing by watching and allowing it. Actually, God is waiting for you to surrender and let Him into your hearts. That is when we will come out on the other side victoriously. He is not standing by watching pain and turmoil betting the odds against your favor. Pain with suffering is of the human condition, for humans create this; therefore, humans will suffer its effects.

Now, one could argue this when you consider natural disasters, and if you read some passages in the Holy Bible, you will even realize that during God's wrath, He often sent some of those natural disasters, for example, as seen in Numbers 16:30-34. He did so as a way to show His judgment against sin. As the creator of the universe, He made the laws of nature and sometimes, natural disasters happen due to the laws of nature. Hurricanes, tornadoes, and typhoons happen as the result of divergent weather patterns colliding. Earthquakes are a result of the earth's plate structure shifting. A tsunami is the result of an underwater earthquake. He allows natural disasters to remind you of His power, to get you to respect nature's sovereignty. He also wants to wake people up, to get them to recognize His goodness and mercy!

I often hear of people cursing God because of these disasters, but I rarely hear these same people praise God for all of the good and calm days they've experienced.

Trauma is inevitable, and no one is immune. But when you accept God as the head of your life, and you lovingly invite Jesus into your heart, you will learn how to get through the trauma, and emerge victoriously just as I did after my trauma.

PTSD is a difficult challenge that requires strong faith in order to meet that challenge and win. It takes remembering who you were before the significant event occurred in your life. If you are born into suffering and experience trauma on a daily basis, and you want to survive the odds, it will take you knowing that God made you from love. That with the love He has for you, He has equipped you with the strength to survive your tough time only if you lean on Him for support and understanding. Once you lean on God for support, you will be able to become resilient and strong.

It takes great faith, prayer, and time to get past PTSD but you can and you will. You might experience some bumps and bruises along the way but you will develop tough skin, and you will have something called a testimony. A testimony is a story unique to you about what you went through. It is usually a story of great resilience and bravery. It is something you will never forget, which will make and mold you into the person that you are to be. It will shape your purpose and give you drive to keep putting one foot in front of the other. My story of how I survived sex trafficking and the atrocity of domestic violence to learn how to love myself and forgive is my testimony. I share it whenever I can to show others what faith in God can do.

In order to recover from PTSD symptoms and trauma, the Creator has blessed some people with unique gifts to help you in addition to His support, so that you can have adequate support on an earthly level. In the upcoming chapters, I'll explain more about the types of things you can do to surpass trauma, and people who can actually help you do this. It will take some work on your part to heal from trauma. It takes knowing that the tough times won't last forever, and that if you persevere, you can come out victorious on the other side.

Prayer for Sufferers of Trauma:

"God, I know that with you all things are possible. I know that with your grace and mercy, I can withstand the current storm to emerge victoriously. Please, give me strength to continue this journey. Amen"

Do I Suffer From Trauma?

A personal trauma assessment is needed to see if we have, in fact, suffered trauma. There are times when we have chosen to forget the pain of our past, and therefore we may feel there is nothing we need to heal. By answering the questions truthfully, you will be able to see if there has been or there is trauma in your life.

Stressful Life Events

Write **YES** or **NO** as the case may be.
1. Have you ever been physically abused as a child by a caregiver, parent, guardian, or other person?
2. Have you ever been physically abused as an adult by a romantic partner, date, family member, stranger, or other person?
3. Are you currently in any physical pain?
4. Have you ever been in a serious accident?
5. Has your life ever been threatened by physical force or by the use of a weapon?
6. Has anyone at any time in your life ever physically forced you to have intercourse, oral or anal, against your wishes or when you were helpless (i.e. asleep, intoxicated, or high)?
7. Has anyone ever tried to touch your body parts against your wishes?
8. Has anyone ever made fun of you or shamed you for your appearance or weight?
9. Have you ever suffered from an eating disorder (i.e. bulimia, anorexia, overeating)

Write **YES** or **NO** as the case maybe:

10. Have you ever witnessed someone else being seriously inured, killed, attacked, sexually assaulted?
11. Have you ever lost someone close to you due to death?
12. Have you experienced a traumatic loss of a pet or animal?
13. Have you ever been discriminated against due to gender, race, sexual orientation, religious beliefs, or social status?
14. Have you ever suffered a loss at the hand of an organized entity (religious, government, police, or social organization)?
15. Have you ever been exposed to a natural disaster?
16. Have you ever had a life-threatening illness?
17. Have you ever suffered from neglect or abandonment by a parent(s)?
18. Has a close friend or family member ever committed suicide?
19. Have you ever been in any other situation where you were seriously injured, or your life was threatened (e.g. military combat or being in a war zone)?
20. Have you ever been in an extremely fighting situation that you have not reported?

After taking this assessment, look over your answers. If you answered yes to any of the above twenty questions, you may be suffering from trauma. It would be wise to hold on to these answers, and show them to one of the *healers* that I'll explain in chapter two, to begin working on your emotional healing.

Chapter 2
Practitioners

"Once you open up to receive help on your trauma symptoms, you can quickly begin to do the work it takes to forgive yourself and others, so as to enjoy a peaceful life."

It is important to note that getting help to overcome the symptoms of trauma and abuse is important if you want to forgive yourself and others that caused trauma in your life. I also want to highlight that there is no reason to feel embarrassed or ashamed for seeking help after surviving trauma. Actually, you are to be applauded. PTSD symptoms are exhausting, and can keep you feeling as if you are trapped in a never-ending cycle of pain and confusion. I can recall the days that I suffered from PTSD. I simply watched the sun rise and set without ever leaving my bedroom. I had no energy. I was completely lethargic and depressed. I had thoughts of suicidal ideation and I truly felt as if my child would have been better off without me in his life. The only reason I fought back for my life was my son. His smile made it bearable and gave me a reason to try. So I know how it feels to get to a very low point in your life.

In order to break free and to reclaim your life, help is needed. You do not have to suffer alone. First, let me point out that you are never alone anyway if you allow Jesus to walk beside you for comfort and support. Once you open up to receive help for your trauma symptoms, you can quickly begin to do the work it takes to forgive yourself and others for an enjoyable and peaceful life. You can mix and match the below healing practices for maximum effectiveness.

Clinicians

I want to tell you that it's not easy going to a professional, sitting in front of such a stranger to bare your soul and share the most intimate stories about your background. I always recommend people to shop around a bit, to make sure the clinician is licensed and has a background in treating trauma. Just because you went to them once or twice doesn't mean you have to stay with them. The relationship between a clinician and the client has to be in sync; otherwise, the client won't be open or receptive to the treatment.

It's also important that you don't feel judged by the clinician. When I owned and operated a behavioral health company, I contracted various licensed clinical therapists to provide mental health assessments and therapy for my trauma clients. At a point in time, I had to sever ties with some of them due to their judgmental and unethical treatment of my clients. It may not seem like a big deal to you, but if a therapist demeans a client for what they've experienced in their past, their decisions, current situations, or even make fun of their names (you'd be surprised), they are not compassionate enough to help a trauma patient. A therapist has to be able to listen intently to his or her patients without passing judgment on them, which should be evident by his or her non-verbal communication, body language, and facial expressions.

My organization PWs provides mentoring to girls who are trauma survivors of sex crimes, sex trafficking, and domestic violence from the ages of 12-18 years old. I have had some of these young clients come back to tell me that their clinicians gasped, or gave them displeasing looks while hearing their stories. Understandably, this would make anyone feel uncomfortable and resistant to treatment.

Personally, I was extremely nervous seeking out clinical help for my own PTSD symptoms because all my life I heard that we, African-Americans, shouldn't sit down in front of strangers to tell our concern. We are told to take our problems to the Lord in prayer. Sometimes, you need more than prayer; sometimes, you need a listening ear to help you sort things out, and someone who will talk things out with you. You need a compassionate person that can give you a sense of direction, and helpful tools to navigate your life. God gave some people the gift of being thoughtful, heart-centered clinicians who are helpful to others in a clinical and therapeutic way. Therefore, you can be rest assured that seeking therapy is fine. Don't fall for the stigma associated with seeking clinical help that if you do, you are crazy. The stigma made me weary of seeking treatment at first because I didn't want to feel or look crazy, but I didn't want to go crazy either from the trauma I suffered in my life. I knew there had to be some relief, and if that meant that people would call me crazy for seeking out clinical help, then oh well!

I began my search and finally settled on a man that I would never have thought in a million years would help me the way that he did. I found a great therapist after my trafficking nightmare. I didn't have health insurance during the time, but after I called the office of my clinician, he made it known that he would take me on a sliding scale fee. I got the directions and set off to meet this man.

My new clinical therapist was an old white man in his seventies; just imagine what my thoughts would be when I first met him. Upon being ushered into his office, I just sat in front of him and stared. He never allowed my non-verbal communication to thwart his mission of getting me to talk to him. Day after day, I just showed up and sat. I didn't say much, maybe just look around his office and stare at his degrees on the way, and the massive amounts of paperwork on his desk. I'd comment on something small like the weather. It took me a good while to open up and talk to this man who looked more like Santa Claus, than a therapist. I had to put my own judgment and pride aside, and he turned out to be exactly who the Creator wanted for me.

I was so afraid of him judging me that I had to stop judging him! I took for granted that our differences would get in the way of him doing his job, but that didn't happen. He helped me get over my PTSD symptoms and even pushed me to write creatively by journaling. In fact, because of his influence, I became a spoken-word artist in my city. I actually recorded an album, and performed around town; and he and his wife would frequent my shows. It was hilarious looking out into this crowd from the stage and seeing him there; he and his wife were sitting at a table enjoying a drink in the midst of hip, urban folks that were in their 20s or 30s. They were there looking like Mr. and Mrs. Claus, clapping the loudest after each song, and giving me a standing ovation. I loved the support and knowing that going to see him, and having him talk to me, made it that much easier for me to continue my recovery.

As the years went on, I ended up seeing different therapists due to other situations. However, thank God for discernment because I knew how to get the heck out of there when the vibe wasn't right, or I felt judged instead of helped. I am telling you this because I want you to understand that it is all up to you. You are in control of who you allow to help you on your healing journey. You are the one who has to spend the money so if it isn't right for you, do not stay, and keep it moving! Do not be afraid to seek clinical help, it is there for us as one of the most important tools to heal.

Life Coaches and Advisors

There are non-clinical people such as life coaches, spiritual directors, spiritual advisors, spiritual counselors, or energy healers who help people heal from trauma as well. They specialize in treating trauma and have been trained to do the work to help a person holistically; mind, body, and soul.

* Life coaches are people who counsel and encourage clients on matters that relate to their careers or personal challenges. I am a life coach for people who are survivors of trauma. It's my specialty since I am a victor over various traumas and I've had various training as it relates to trauma and sexual exploitation.

* A spiritual director has had training in a church discipline or spiritual life. He is a person who has very close knowledge of the person's spirit, who is seeking direction. This type of help should be done in person, not over the phone or via the Internet. The person seeking help has to be open and revealing with their past, present, and concerns. He or she must be willing to do as he or she is told as it relates to their spirit.

* A spiritual advisor gives spiritual advice to the person while a spiritual counselor will counsel a person on a specific problem or aspect of that person's spiritual life.

* An energy healer works directly with the energetic level of the person seeking help. This person acknowledges that everything is energy, and seeks to rectify the disruption within that person's energy field. He/she uses energy medicine, energy therapy, energy healing, and even spiritual help by focusing on "holistic" healing. Holistic means "wholistic" healing of the person; not just pinpointing the illness and treating it. The healer's primary focus is to heal the whole person so the individual can live a healthier way of life, with peace and balance being the focus. He or she does this in various ways such as working with Reiki, sound therapy, crystals, chakra work, auras, and prana.

I received clinical help in the past and I will say that I have never liked taking medications for the symptoms of my trauma. Why? It's because I felt that the medicine prescribed was just for the intended illness but never dealt with the root cause. Yes, I had a psychiatrist and psychologist but I needed to go deeper. After researching alternative methods, I found that holistic healers and energy healers had a positive effect on my overall emotional wellbeing, and physical body more than the traditional clinical help did. I believe in energy healing so much that I decided to take up a career in energy work, get certified, and offer this healing to others. I am in no way telling you to forgo a clinical therapist because doing so would prove reckless. And since I am not a clinician, I can't do that, especially since there are instances where prescribing medication to someone suffering from trauma symptoms is absolutely critical in helping them control the symptoms and receive relief.

In my behavioral health business, I worked with clients who were clinically diagnosed with psychiatric disorders due to the trauma they endured. In this case, a clinician is paramount in that person's healing. Psychiatrists and psychologists offer a way to properly diagnose, and clinically treat a person who has been affected psychologically with medication. They have the proper education to mentally assess and treat the client if this is the case. This is why I say it's always best to go see them first, then discuss it with them about your interest in seeing a non-traditional healer. This is important because if you have been diagnosed and given prescribed medication, you shouldn't remove yourself from medication all by yourself without any professional advice. This can be dangerous and even fatal. Removal from medication has to be done under the direction of a clinician.

Many people have been diagnosed with mental illness and are in need of medication to manage these illnesses. There is nothing wrong with taking your medication and pairing it with a non-traditional healer. Together, the combination can bring calm, balance, and order to your life. Together, they offer certain techniques in an effort to heal you holistically.

I am just telling you that for *me* personally, I did not enjoy *not* feeling my feelings! I remember when I was on psychotropic medication to treat my anxiety and depression. I ran into an old friend who told me that her mother had recently passed away. I stood there emotionless, with a plastered smile on my face, saying an upbeat, "Oh I'm sorry about that, do you want to go get a drink and catch up sometime?" Needless to say, the drink never happened, and we lost touch, *again*. Can you blame her? I must have looked like a Stepford wife standing there smiling while she was in tears. I was so embarrassed! That was the day I decided to research alternatives to medications. I hated not being able to feel anything. I was happy no matter what was going on inside of me. I couldn't cry even if I wanted to. The medication also kept me up all hours of the night due to one of its side effects, insomnia. Again, this was my experience, and what prompted me to venture outside of the norm.

I believe that it's important to listen to your body, and by staying in tune with it, you will be able to see how it responds best. Therefore, look into all types of help. The person(s) you choose has to be knowledgeable, supportive, caring, and kind. The person should be a good listener and want to see you get better. Do your research and get the help that you deserve.

After suffering from trauma, I sought:

* Clinical therapy from

_____

It helped me heal. Yes/No (circle one)

* Non-traditional therapy from

_____

It helped me heal. Yes/No (circle one)

In all, I need to seek additional treatment for healing. Yes/No (circle one)

Chapter 3
Healing Practices

Exercise

Physical activity is essential to remove your focus from the pain of trauma and increase your motivation. Many people suffer from a lack of motivation while suffering from PTSD.

When I suffered from PTSD, I took tiny steps on the path to healing by doing physical activity; I first started by simply walking around in my neighborhood. To be able to get moving, utilizing my arms and legs felt great and really redirected my energy. I'll be honest and say that, on some days, I didn't even want to get out of my bed, let alone leave my house. It took sheer willpower to move my body parts. I'm serious! The conversations went something like this in my head, *Toshia, move your legs. Toshia, brush your teeth, take a shower, and comb your hair. Okay good, now put on some clothes, and go for a walk.* This is seriously the conversation I'd have with myself on most days. I was seriously depressed and had to be my own life coach. I didn't know it then, but it's exactly what I was doing. Although it took me a while to even gather up the courage to leave my home, and face society, when I did, I felt better. I eventually made it to a gym and started a routine of working out. I loved the results, and liked what it did for my mind.

Nature

Enjoying nature is extremely therapeutic. Getting off the grid without being immersed in computers, tablets, or phones is healthy for your mind. There is nothing like getting out and enjoying the fresh green grass, the snow in the mountains, or the sound of the ocean waves hitting the tide on a beach. I love to rent a hotel room and stay overnight on the beach listening to the sounds of the ocean waves, and smelling the salt in the air. The sounds of nature can calm and relax your psyche. I am also an avid trail walker and an amateur hiker; I mostly hike in Utah and in the mountains of Nevada. I like to lead hikes for my clients who are trauma survivors. The majestic mountains, animals, rugged terrain, mountain springs, and clean fresh air usually do wonders to their mood. Nature connects you to the Divine on the most intimate level. When I lived in Nevada years ago, afflicted with trauma and feeling lost, I never knew about the beauty that surrounded me. I was so caught up in my own life problems and a seemingly bad life that I was oblivious to the wonderful landscape that laid before me. If you could take some time to put your own problems aside for just one day, to get out into nature to take it all in, you would see that your problems are insignificant compared to God's regal landscape. Let me share with you a personal story of how nature brings clarity and healing.

Very recently, I was dealt a hard blow to my reality. My son who was only nineteen years old at the time, and a college student informed me that I was going to be a grandmother. Unable to wrap my head around this revelation, my feelings were all over the place. Immediately, I blamed myself, which is silly because I have always talked to him about the dangers of unprotected sex, or having sex in general before having a real commitment like marriage. In fact, I went as far as purchasing him condoms! Okay, you get the drift; I just really didn't want to become a grandmother at an early age. So when he and his girlfriend told me the news, I got so upset I just flew off the handle. I then got angry with the girl. I thought to myself who was this girl who had singlehandedly ruined my son's life (unfair treatment, I know, but it's how I felt at the time). I turned the anger towards my son, for not being careful enough. How could he do this to himself? He was too immature to bring a child into the world at such an early age, but not only that, with barely a college education, and no job. I was devastated.

I truly grieved for my son's future that I had already planned. You see, my child was a straight A student, who went to a magnet school throughout his middle and high school years. He had never gotten into any trouble, and as far as I knew, he wanted the same things that I wanted for him— have a college education, play college basketball, and have a successful career in medicine. I had expectations, and I placed my son on a pedestal. Because I had never (and I do mean never) had any problems with him while he was growing up, so I didn't expect this at all. I was side swiped and knocked down, with the air taken out of me.

I must have cried on and off for about a week, and I was barely able to speak to anyone. I didn't want anyone to know about my failure as a parent. I didn't want anyone to know my son was a teen father. I became angry with his own father because he wasn't there for me at such a critical moment, he wasn't there to talk to my son about this, and he just wasn't there at all. So I had the tough job of holding a young man up, who was being forced to become a man, someone else's father, all too quickly. I had to pray, and I mean pray hard to ask for strength. I practiced the *Green Light of Forgiveness* meditation and was finally able to rid myself of the anger. But my son wasn't doing well with the news that he was going to be a father. He looked ill, rarely ate, and crept into a dangerous depression. It wasn't until my mother brought to my attention the following, "Toshia, you do this for a living. You have helped hundreds of girls deal with the reality of teenage motherhood. Yet you are unwilling to help your own?" That is when I snapped out of it, and realized that I had to help my son accept and prepare for the birth of his son at the tender age of 19. At one particular point, he was really scaring us with talks of not being worthy, about being a failure, and not being sure if he had a point to go on living. So, mentor Toshia kicked into overdrive and I told him to pack a backpack, and get his sturdiest shoes, because we were going hiking.

I wanted my son to reconnect with nature because I know how it feels to get knocked off one's feet, to be thrown a curveball in life, the fear of being judged, and to experience trauma. But I also told him that God makes no mistakes, and that his son had purpose just like he had one; and for that reason alone, he needed to get grounded.

We set out for Utah, Zion National Park. My son had never gone hiking before, and he was up for anything if that meant he would feel a little bit better. While driving the four hours to Utah, I saw his demeanor soften, and his jawbone relaxed; and he opened up to me like never before. I played him some motivating music, and we sang songs together just like we did when he was younger. When we arrived at the park, I saw him take in the majestic mountains, the fresh air, and God's beautiful landscape. On the hiking trail, my son and I bonded; and he realized that no matter what, I had his back. We both accepted that our lives, but mostly his, would change forever. On that hike, my son forgave himself, and he quietly planned on the steps he needed to take to be a positive and active part of his child's life. On that hike, we breathed, took mindful steps, and connected to nature in more ways than we imagined. I watched my son meditate while walking, I watched him look at the sky the way he used to as a child—full of wonder and hope. My son took away strength from that hike, which he didn't have before, and even though he never said it verbally, as his mother, I knew he'd be all right.

That is what nature can do for you; it can give you the support you need, and simultaneously heal you at an emotional level.

Eating Healthy

Eating healthy is critical when you are suffering from trauma. During my time of healing, I made the decision to become a vegan. I hardly had the desire to eat anyway, but with my research, I just felt better not eating meat during that time. I even went as far as working at an organic grocery store. During that time, I acclimated myself to different foods that could boost my serotonin levels. Serotonin is a brain chemical that helps send messages throughout your nervous system. This neurotransmitter is produced in our digestive tracts. Serotonin wields powerful influence over many functions like emotions, memory, moods, sleeping habits, and appetites. When your serotonin levels are too low, you experience suicidal thoughts, anxiety, depression, obsessive-compulsive disorders, and all sorts of emotional and behavioral symptoms.

It's important to eat a balanced diet, and it would be great to pair that with essential vitamins that can help.

Vitamins, Herbs

I usually take vitamin B complex, and when I forget to take it, I can really tell the difference. Vitamin B6 supports the production and function of serotonin, melatonin, and dopamine in the brain. I also incorporated the herb, St. Johns Wort, which is effective on mild to moderate depression symptoms. Vitamins Thiamine and folic acid also affect serotonin.

Fish, Poultry, Meat

I have since incorporated meat back in my diet. Whenever I choose to eat some type of meat, I only eat poultry and fish. Mackerel, halibut, salmon, sardines, herring, snapper, and fresh tuna are high in tryptophan and they offer a great source of serotonin. Turkey and chicken are a source of tryptophan as well, and very necessary for serotonin to stay at a reasonable level. If you are a red meat eater, then you will want to incorporate beef, lamp, and liver to provide amino acids and other nutrients to help facilitate the creation of serotonin.

Don't worry, my vegan friends, as long as you get your protein in by eating plenty of nuts, seeds, grains that are rich in vitamin B, essential oils with omega-3 fatty acids, fruits, vegetables, legumes, and beans, you're all good.

The point is to eat healthy and eliminate or minimize the amount of fat, sugar, and alcohol you consume. Avoid smoking as well. You can boost your serotonin and elevate your mood naturally!

Yoga

Yoga is a wonderful exercise that actually heals you mentally, spiritually, and physically. This form of physical mediation originated in India over 5,000 years ago. I started taking yoga very early after my ordeal, and it was daunting at first to walk into a class that had people who thought they were human pretzels. No, in all seriousness, I have seen people contort their bodies into all kinds of positions that I didn't think were humanly possible. I am not the most limber person but I do all right. Although it isn't all about how well you can move your body into the positions, it's about breath control, meditation, and the connection to the *divine*. There is a certain, required degree of discipline to the practice, and you can get better over time. Many people go to yoga unable to sit Indian style on the floor; but with continued practice, you will be able to ease into positions in no time. Yoga has been widely accepted by Westerners now. The military has even adopted its practice as a form of healing for the soldiers that come back from war to help heal their PTSD symptoms. Yoga is a personal journey, and it's about patience and being gentle with yourself—exactly what is needed when you have survived trauma.

Eye Movement Desensitization and Reprocessing (EMDR)

"EMDR quickly opens new windows on reality, allowing people to see solutions within themselves that they never knew were there. And it's a therapy where the client is very much in charge, which can be particularly meaningful when people are recovering from having their power taken away by abuse and violation."
Laura S. Brown, Ph.D.

EMDR is a psychotherapy developed by American psychologist and educator Francine Shapiro, PhD, which emphasizes disturbing memories as the cause of mental or behavioral disorders. It is used to help deal with the symptoms of PTSD. EMDR therapy is described as a cost-effective, non-invasive, and evidence-based method of psychotherapy that facilitates adaptive information processing. EMDR therapy is an eight-phase treatment that lengthily identifies and addresses experiences that have overwhelmed the brain's natural resilience or coping capacity, and have thereby generated traumatic symptoms and/or harmful coping strategies. It is by this identification and the EMDR therapy that the patients are able to reprocess traumatic information until it is no longer psychologically disruptive. The treatment approach targets past experience, triggers, and even future thoughts of potential future challenges. It alleviates the presenting symptoms, and decreases or eliminates distress from the disturbing memory. The person emerges with an improved sense of self, relief from present and future anticipated triggers.

Progressive Muscle Relaxation (PMR)

Progressive Muscle Relaxation or PMR is an exercise done to loosen up muscle tension within the body. You do so by progressively tensing and relaxing muscle groups throughout your entire body from your feet to the top of your head, one group at a time. This technique is self-administered, and easy to do. It was created by E. Jacobson and introduced in 1938. This exercise is used to help combat stress when used consecutively over time. You can even assist your body in relaxing for a more restful sleep.

It is important that you only relax one body part at a time. You will also need to take care as not to overexert your muscles; you can do this by listening to your body. Listening to it tells you when you are exerting enough tension in a certain area, to prevent injury. This is especially important if you are already sore or experiencing discomfort in a particular area.

Focus on each body part by tightening for a count of five, and then releasing that body part for a count of five. Here are the body parts that you will need to focus on tightening and relaxing at a regular interval:

Right foot
Right calf
Right thigh
Left foot
Left ankle
Left calf
Left thigh
Buttocks
Back
Stomach
Chest
Right hand and wrist
Right arm
Left hand and wrist
Left arm
Shoulder
Neck
Face
Scalp

Practice this when there are no interruptions, including music, television, or cellular devices. Complete silence is help

Tapping

The emotional freedom technique (EFT) or tapping as it is generally called is a psychological acupressure technique.
Tapping is a mixture of ancient Chinese acupressure and Modern Psychology. Tapping quickly gets to the heart of your issue, working to rewire the brain, and the amygdala—the region of the brain associated with emotions specifically—to create safety in the body and release trauma. Tapping is extremely effective in the letting go, and practicing of forgiveness.

When I first heard of tapping, I was at a meditation circle. The instructor told us that we would start tapping to release any emotional blockages and stress. I leaned over to the lady sitting next to me with my nose scrunched up and whispered, "Tapping, what are we gonna be tapping on?" The lady didn't appreciate my ignorance and just rolled her eyes and ignored me. So I watched the instructor go into how we were going to tap away our life's problems and get emotionally free. *Yeah okay*, I thought as I rolled my eyes. I went along with it since I didn't want to appear to be the oddball in the group. She had us repeat certain affirmations while we were tapping. It was there I learned the following affirmation,
"Even though I feel _____, I still love and appreciate myself." You just have to fill in the blank with whatever bothers, or ails you at the time. We tapped on the top of our heads, in the middle of our brow, on our temples, underneath our eyes, underneath our nose right above our top lip,

underneath our bottom lip, on the collarbone, underneath the arm on our side, and finally on the side of our hand.

After we finished tapping, I said my goodbye to everyone and eagerly left. As I was walking, I felt emotions begin to well up inside of me. I felt lighter, and very free. I literally floated out of the studio, glided towards my car, got in, sat behind the wheel, and bawled my eyes out. I mean, snot nosed, ugly crying. I didn't understand why I was crying so hard and for what reason. I wasn't upset, nor was I crying about anything in particular. It felt like some cleansing. I looked up and out of my car window, I noticed the woman that was sitting next to me in class opening her car door, and she gave me a knowing smile before she cranked up and drove away. I learned the power of tapping that day; I drove away feeling 10lbs lighter and emotionally free. Crying isn't typically an effect that happens after a EFT session, but everyone reacts to tapping differently. To this day, I use tapping anytime I need to get clear, or deal with any stress. It is a simple technique; it is quick and easy to learn. I have taught my 9-year old to tap whenever she feels anxiety or sadness due to the absence of her father. While tapping, she says the following, "*Although my father is absent, I will not allow it to affect me negatively, I love and forgive him. I deeply love and appreciate myself.*" By teaching her this affirmation, and the tapping technique, I was able to give her essential self-soothing techniques to utilize on the spot, whenever needed. She now feels empowered, safe, and in control of her emotions. Please, watch my tapping video at *greenlightofforgiveness.com.*

Essential Oils

Essential oils are a huge part of my every day regimen, and I utilize them in my spirituality coaching practice as well. The International Organization for Standardization

(ISO) in their Vocabulary of Natural Materials (ISO/D1S9235.2) defines an essential oil as a product made by distillation with either water or steam or by mechanical processing of citrus rinds or by dry distillation of natural materials. Following the distillation, the essential oil is physically separated from the water phase. Trauma leaves a stamp on people's emotions, and in my opinion, it leaves the emotions bruised and battered the same way a person would have physical bruises after being involved in a physical fight. Instead, trauma is a fight within the mind. When a person suffers from physical bruises, you nurse those wounds with salves, ointments, medication, etc. Therefore, you need something natural to help heal the bruises of the emotions. You can do so with essential oils. I have an oil for any emotional situation that arises in my life. I utilize them to raise my vibration and energy level. My absolute favorite, which I use to raise my vibration is, Elevation™ by doTERRA. I also use the oils to raise the vibration in my home and to make my home smell wonderful with the help of a diffuser. These natural oils are non-toxic and all natural. I use oils when I practice energy healing on my clients. Each client has specific problems that we target, which require specific oils.

For the purpose of this book, I want to discuss specific oils to treat emotional and spiritual problems. There are varieties of brands that offer them. I can only speak on the oils that I have researched thoroughly and currently use. I don't believe in synthetic or watered-down oils. The oils used to treat trauma must be pure. For trauma healing, I prefer Young Living's SARA.™ SARA™ is an empowering blend of therapeutic-grade essential oils designed to help soothe deep emotional wounds. It can help individuals release negative emotional blocks and begin recovery from the traumatic memory of sexual or ritual torment and other forms of physical or emotional abuse. I've used it on my clients who suffer from those specific trauma symptoms. Some essential oils like frankincense and lavender can help you relax your body and mind, and put you into a meditative state. Take care to check if you are allergic to these oils before placing them onto your skin. As an alternative to placing it directly on your skin, it helps to put a couple of drops on a cotton ball and inhale the aroma. Do your research on the oils that may be right for you.

Journal

Journaling is powerful. Writing down how you feel offers a relief when you know your thoughts and observations are coming out of your head, and going somewhere, even if it is just on paper. Journaling is the practice of keeping a diary or journal where you record thoughts and feelings surrounding the events going on in your life. It preserves your memories, improves your writing, and sharpens your intelligence. This practice is therapeutic as it helps to relieve stress. It always helps to be able to reread what you've written, and to see how far you've evolved as a person. I often employ journaling to save my life. While experiencing trauma, I was able to get out all my feelings on paper without holding back. This is one helpful tool I teach my clientele to do and continue well after we no longer work together.

Creativity

We are all talented at something, even if you don't know it yet. For me, God gave me the talent to write and sing. So every time I bring up the subject of creative writing, it warms my heart deeply. When I was a little girl, I read any and every book I could get my hands on. In fact, when I was around the age of 8, I wrote my very first book, *Cindy and her Maracas*. At the age of 10, I won a contest for reading the most books in the state of Illinois! This is where my love for the written word stems from. I used to get lost in books as a child, as it offered a wonderful escape. Therefore, my mind was made up that when I grew up, I was going to be an author. Of course, it didn't come into fruition until much later, but it happened. Some of my clients write poetry or short stories. They draw, paint, perform spoken poems, and dance. Whatever feels good to you is what you should do. Immediately after my trauma, I wrote a book of fiction that I entitled, *High Stakes,* it is available on Amazon.com. I didn't self-publish it until 2011. I wasn't ready to write my life's story but I did want to write about the underworld of Las Vegas, Nevada. The book did quite well, as I went on a virtual book tour, had a book signing, and went on a local news show in Memphis, Tennessee to promote it. I set up a vendor table at a few book fairs as well. Prior to that, I wrote poetry to escape my depression and PTSD in the early 2000's. I even garnered up enough courage to start performing at open mic nights and eventually, I teamed up with a local producer in Memphis, Tennessee where I recorded these poems as songs. Today, you can Google my music and my one-and-only album entitled, *Open Book*—it's available for purchase. I used my voice to sing, and talk about the things that most mattered to me, while providing a place for healing for myself. No one knew it at the time, but it was my therapy, and I had no fear while on the stage singing.

    The point of telling you all of this is, it doesn't matter what you do, just find a creative outlet that feels good to you. I get my clients to share their creative gifts as a part of their own healing process. I find that some start to look forward to drawing, painting, and/or writing. The point is to start opening up. You can choose to share your truth or not. But get creative; it will help in your healing process. It's a great release when you are working toward practicing forgiveness.

There are multitudes of ways to jumpstart your healing process. If you combine one of these healing modalities in addition to clinical and non-traditional help, you are well on your way to removing the roadblocks to forgiveness.

Below is a simple prayer to assist you on your journey toward healing from PTSD:

"Creator, I ask that you direct my footsteps on my pathway to healing from trauma. I ask that you give me discernment to choose a competent and reputable clinician or alternative healer. Please, help me to open my mind and heart to accept the support and strength and energy to help in my own healing process. Amen."

Spirituality & Religion

"In this you rejoice, though now for a little while, if necessary, you have been grieved by various trials, so that the tested genuineness of your faith—more precious than gold that perishes though it is tested by fire—may be found to result in praise and glory and honor at the revelation of Jesus Christ" 1 Peter 1:6-7.

Leaning on your spiritual or religious beliefs during a rough time proves priceless in the healing process of trauma. In my opinion, there is little more comfort than being able to go to your place of worship and being supported by other compassionate members. If you currently belong to a religion, now is the perfect time to reach out to someone in a position to help you sort out your feelings, and give you spiritual counseling. They are there to comfort and be a shoulder for you to lean on. In most religions, you can consult with leadership, and they will direct you to those passages within your religious texts, which serve as a footprint on what to do and what the Creator says about the particular thing you are experiencing.

If you are spiritual, you may not practice any specific religion or you may practice a combination of religious practices all at once, such as Christianity, Buddhism, Sikhism, or Islam—the list can go on and on. As a spiritual person, you acknowledge that there is a Higher Power, and you simply do what you know is right within. You lead with love, with the base being compassion for self and others. You cause no harm, and you offer your gifts unto the world, to make the sphere of humankind existence a better place. While this book is a guide for you to heal from trauma and practice the *Green Light of Meditation*, I would be remiss in not telling you where this all culminated from. This is a great time to tell you how my own spiritual enlightenment happened.

After my trafficking ordeal, I became withdrawn from society; I merely laid around the house, zoning out on television, and feeling sorry for myself. I wallowed in self-pity, and victimization had me in a death grip by my throat. I did not leave home unless I had to take my son to school, or pick him up, or attend therapy appointments. Whenever I had the energy, I would do some sort of physical activity. Other than that, I was holed up in my room at my parents' home, reading. I read any and everything I could about religion. I had an insatiable appetite of learning about God and trying to find out my purpose in life. I needed to find out if what I learned during my younger years in church were actually true. I never really connected to "God," and after suffering trauma, what little connection I had was long gone. I read mostly books on Buddhism and Christianity.

One day while I journeyed out to a bookstore, a particular book stood out to me, *Conversations with God* by Neale Donald Walsch. I bought it with no real expectations. I took it home and read it morning, noon, and night. I was simply amazed that this man claimed that God spoke to him and directed him to write his book. Needless to say, I kept an open mind and became enthralled, gulping up the content line by line. I had begun my journey with meditation during this time of studying religion. I had no idea of what I was doing, other than sitting in Indian style with my eyes closed, and being quiet. It was hard to keep my mind still and quiet because I would often replay what happened to me. I could see the faces of the men who hurt me, and my meditation sessions would often end with me in tears, feeling angry. This one particular night while I was supposed to still my mind and not think of anything, once more I spoke to God in my mind and told Him that I wasn't happy with Him. I expressed how much I hated the way my life turned, how I thought He didn't love me because of all the trauma I experienced. Pretty much, I told God He could shove it! Now this is where it gets really freaky. When I questioned God for allowing me to suffer, I heard a male voice (which is why I call God a He), and He simply said, "I love you, Toshia." It was distinct, and extremely pronounced. I felt a very warm and loving feeling rush through me. I opened my eyes, and looked around my room. I started to freak out because I thought maybe the perpetrator who kidnapped me broke into the house and was back for revenge to make me pay for leaving. As I frantically searched the room, the voice in my head said it again, and it added, "Trust me." My body started trembling, and my breathing became erratic. Again the voice said, "I love you, I saved you, do not be afraid."

Let me just tell you now that I ran out of my bedroom, down the hall, and I went to my parents and woke my mother up out of her sleep. I told her that in the morning I needed her to take me to the mental hospital because I had lost my mind. My mother asked me what was wrong and I told her that I was hearing voices and that I needed to be admitted. My mother became silent and beckoned for me to join her in the bed. Yes, my big grown ass jumped in that bed and made my mother cuddle me. She proceeded to ask me a few more questions and then simply said one thing,

"Toshia, peace be still."

She repeated it once more, "Toshia, peace be still."

Confused, I asked her, "What mommy?"

"Be still child. That is the Lord talking to you."

I didn't ask any more questions but that night I slept like a baby; I slept for a long time fully at peace. From that night forward, I became quiet. I listened to the voice, and I allowed it to tell me that I had a purpose, that I had a reason to live. That voice told me that I would be doing something miraculous for people in this world. That voice was right.

Prayer

Prayer is at the very cornerstone of my spiritual practice. I believe in finding solace in the bosom of the lover of my soul, my peacekeeper in prayer, Jesus Christ. I think of prayer as an act of talking to Jesus while meditation is listening to Him. To me, there is a very distinct difference. If you are not a believer in a Higher Power, you can still pray. You can still bow your head, close your eyes, bring your palms together close to your heart (chest), and simply offer gratitude to the *universe* within your mind.

Here is a prayer to say for guidance:

"God, I come to you now humbly with an open heart. I ask that you restore my faith. I come before you with a bruised and battered heart. I want to be made whole again. I pray that you assist in this healing. Amen."

Healing Techniques

Locate the type of healing practices you currently do and in the empty column notate the frequency in which you practice each.

	Days a week
EMDR	
PMR	
Journaling	
Yoga	
Essential Oils (which one do you use?)	
Meditation	
Prayer	
Walking	
Jogging	
Other Exercises (What Type?)	

Journaling	
Creativity (What Type)	

Do you see a pattern of behavior here in relationship to your healing? Are you currently physically active? If you have not started on a physical activity, now is a great time to start. In doing so, you have a hand in your own healing.

Chapter 4
Energy Healing

Clearing the Path: Chakra Balancing

Although energy healing is a method of healing trauma, I would like to present a few methods in a separate chapter. I truly believe in the power of energy healing and I practice it on the clients that are open to it or seek it out exclusively. I have seen how it can totally change a person's life dramatically, including my own. I had a client named Denise who came to me for some energy healing work. She disclosed that she did not have a belief system and, in fact, she felt disassociated from the Divine. She stated she didn't believe in a Higher Power because if there were a God (as she put it), it wouldn't have allowed such bad things to happen to her.

I see this more often than not with my clients, and it is completely understandable. How can I ask someone to simply forgive, and believe in an Almighty Ruler, when they have suffered unimaginable things? I get it, and I understand it. In order to help Denise on her pathway to forgiveness, I had to clear and balance her *chakras* to get them to work in harmony with one another. The danger of not having your chakras balanced is that it will lead to discord within every area of your life. Let me explain each of the seven main chakras and how they can affect you if they are not balanced

The Chakra System

The chakra system deals with the energy systems in our bodies, where energy flows through. There are said to be many chakras but seven main chakras are the life-force energy centers within our bodies. The word chakra is Sanskrit, which means wheel. When translated from the Hindi language, it means wheel of spinning energy. They spin like vortexes or wheels of color. I will explain each one as follows:

Root Chakra

This is the first chakra and it sits at the base of your spine; it's the survival center. This chakra is associated with the color red. This root chakra is all about safety; and when left unbalanced, you worry about your safety and money, you could have a food disorder, and perhaps your living environment is unstable. Denise was a complete worrywart, and very hyperactive. She constantly apologized; worried that she would offend me, and could not sit still. She denied herself of working on her dreams for fear that she would not be able to take care of her daughter or herself.

Sacral Chakra

The second chakra is associated with the color orange and sits just two inches below you navel. This chakra deals with our ability to honor others. If this chakra is unbalanced, you might be cold emotionally and have sexual problems. If you have ever experienced sexual abuse, this chakra is most affected. Some problems I have seen in prior clients include sexual dysfunction, sexual addictions, sexual and reproductive issues, back pain, fear, and emotional unavailability. One of my male clients, Anthony came to me for six weeks of professional help because his fiancée left him, owing to the fact that he was emotionally unavailable. She stated that he was cold, and had total disregard for her feelings. Later on, I found out that all of his past relationships ended abruptly due to the same reason. He never got healed from the emotional trauma he experienced as a child. We had to balance his second chakra in order to proceed with the *Green Light of Forgiveness*.

Solar Plexus Chakra

The third chakra is yellow, and sits three inches above your navel. People with these blockages have self-esteem problems, fear of rejection, and depression. They have no self-respect, self-love, self-worth, or self-compassion. Melissa came to see me because of self-esteem problems. She felt as if she were watching her life pass her by. She hated her job, and hadn't been on a date in over two years! When I met her, the first thing I noticed upon meeting her is how she couldn't even give me eye contact. She sat with her hands in her lap fidgeting. I asked her to name some things that she liked about herself, and the only things she could come up with were tangible things. Denise looked at me and said, "I like my hair, my clothes, and my car." I remember saying, "No, I mean what do you like about yourself? Personality? What are some good things about you?" She just hung her head, and tears streamed down her cheeks. If you are struggling with loving yourself, this chakra will need to be balanced.

Heart Chakra

The fourth chakra is green, and associated with the heart, which prompted me to develop the *Green Light of Forgiveness* program. When the heart chakra is blocked, you could experience the absence of joy, gratitude, compassion, and love. You also feel unworthy, or the polar opposite of loving too much. I have seen situations where people are clingy within their intimate relationships, and suffocating their loved ones. They also feel jealousy, fear due to being alone, anger, resentment, bitterness, and hatefulness. Victims feel powerless, and feel they have to take what they can get, as if they do not deserve better. I experienced this for the longest time. I sabotaged potential relationships in my past with men that I thought would never accept my past, or love me for who I was. I suffered because I honestly didn't think I deserved better. I didn't have any compassion for myself. I blamed myself for the trauma that I experienced. So anytime anyone wanted to get close to me, I pushed them away for fear that I was just going to mess it up. I ended up settling in a loveless marriage, and being completely miserable.

People who have been involved in abusive relationships, or watched violence while growing up in their homes, have strong feelings of guilt or shame. The feeling of powerlessness is at the center of their being. There are no feelings of forgiveness when this chakra is blocked, and virtually no trust within relationships.

Throat Chakra

The fifth chakra is located at the throat and deals with communication and self-expression. People whose throat chakra is blocked have a hard time speaking up for themselves. They can be liars, secretive, and not able to express themselves verbally. They may have been verbally abused, or be verbally abusive to themselves and others. For a person who habitually gossips, his or her fifth chakra is blocked. Prior to the speech I gave at TEDx Fremont Women, in Las Vegas, Nevada, *The Pact*, in 2013, my throat chakra was completely blocked. In fact, I suffered from major sinus infections that would lay me flat on my back! I'm talking being bed ridden. I had no idea why I couldn't get rid of these infections; I literally would see a doctor for the same problem every year. Ever since I stood on stage and delivered my speech about my past, stood in my truth, and stopped living in shame by keeping my past a secret, I have not suffered from any sinus or throat infections! I cleared my throat chakra and got free.

Third Eye Chakra

The sixth chakra sits in between the eyebrows in the middle of the forehead. When this chakra is blocked, the person has an inability to see other's points of views. They may be a person with the *way or the highway* point of view. They may be closed minded, cold, manipulative, domineering, authoritarian, and religiously dogmatic. This person may also have a hard time focusing, lack clarity, be easily confused, and live in a fantasy world. This person may also suffer from mental illness. Amanda had a hard time focusing, which caused problems at work. She lacked clarity, and was not easy to talk to due to her seeing only her point of view, from victimization. She needed to clear her third eye chakra in order to be open to seeing another's point of view. If not, she was in jeopardy of losing her executive position at work, and even some personal friendships.

Crown Chakra

The seventh chakra sits at the top of your head and deals with spirituality. Remember when I said Denise had no connection to a Higher Power? She rejected any notion of spirituality. This chakra took the longest to clear in our session. When this chakra is blocked, people tend to suffer from headaches, confusion, depression, and sensitivity to light and sound. They ignore their inner voice, and operate completely out of fear.

If you can identify with any of these symptoms, it means one or more of your chakras are unbalanced or even worst blocked. You can get them clear by working from the bottom, at the root, up to the crown chakra. You must learn how to meditate first in order to clear and cleanse these chakras. It is a great idea to learn visualization and affirmations to get them aligned and healed. If you want information on how to clear your chakras, go and watch my videos on how to clear and balance your chakras at greenlightofforgiveness.com and select this option under healing modalities.

Reiki

I have always known that there was energy in the laying of the hands. Laying of hands has been heavily utilized in religious practices and spirituality for centuries. I first heard of laying of the hands in the Bible. Jesus practiced laying on of hands to heal people. So when I first heard of Reiki, I wasn't too surprised that it involved the laying of the hands. But when I attended my "Reiki I" training class, I found that it is much more than that. In fact, what I learned and experienced gave me a whole other appreciation for this ancient Japanese practice. The word *Reiki* is made of two Japanese words—Rei which means "God's Wisdom or the

Higher Power" and Ki which is "life force energy." So Reiki is actually "God's higher power of life force energy." It is a method for stress reduction and relaxation, which also promotes healing. In fact, you don't have to touch the person at all. There is validity that you don't have to be near a person to heal them. You can send anyone healing energy. In Reiki, you would have to get the person you wish to heal permission, but it works just as good as if they were lying down in front of you. I took Reiki I, II, and Reiki Master training by my Reiki Master, Brenda Calvin, wherein she explained Reiki thoroughly and completely. Upon meeting her, I just knew that she embodied this life force energy that God gifted her. She saw a natural talent in me that I possessed, and I felt it while I practiced on my classmates. Today, I practice Reiki on clientele at their request, and have even practiced long distance. Again, although it is seen as the laying of hands, you don't actually have to lay hands on the person for it to be effective. You simply have to tap into this life force energy and have permission from the person whom you seek to heal. The intention is to create deep relaxation, to help speed healing, reduce pain, and decrease other symptoms a person may be experiencing. If you are interested in this healing modality, ensure you hire a person who has received proper training in this energy healing. The techniques and symbols used to become attuned so as to perform this energy healing work have to be done only by someone who has been attuned themselves and certified to do so. Reiki has become widely accepted and some healthcare settings have even invited Reiki practitioners into the operating rooms. It has been proven that Reiki is one of the leading forms of energy healing in hospitals, clinics, and private practices.

Here is a prayer for your energy healer:

"God, I ask that you anoint the hands that assist in my healing. Please come through them and use them as your vessel to help me heal. Amen."

Chakra Check

In the diagram below, indicate which chakra you are having problems with. Use the space to write what those particular problems are. Once identified, you will be able to work to resolve them. You can also take this diagram to an energy healer so they can have a better understanding of where to help you unblock certain chakras.

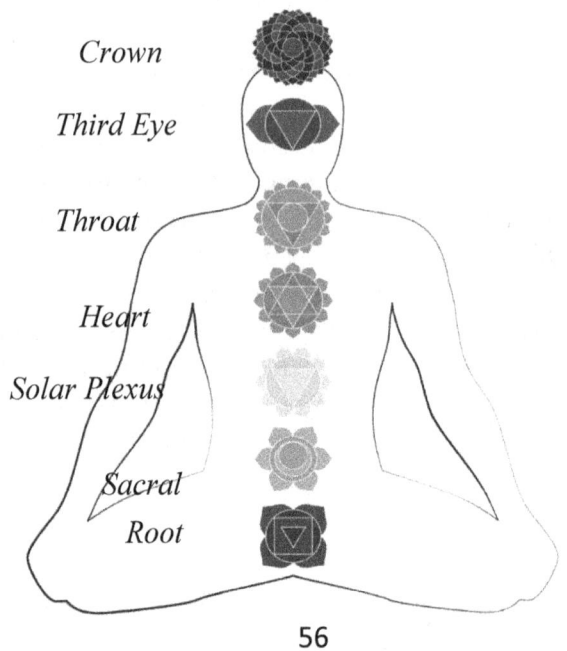

Chapter

5
The Pain of Remembering

"The discomfort of remembering keeps many people silent, and that silence represses the memory."

I remember giving a talk at a university and immediately upon exiting the stage, a woman named Jessica approached me and eagerly took my business card. As soon as I retired to my hotel room and fired up my laptop to check my inbox, I had an email from her awaiting me. I read the message and empathized with her regarding her pain and frustration. Jessica explained that she was a 46-year-old professional woman who had trouble trusting others because of the pain she endured during her childhood days. Her stepfather sexually molested Jessica over a 5-year period. Although he was sentenced and went to jail for the crime, the relationship with her mother was ruined. Jessica stated that her mother blamed her for her stepfathers' incarceration and for the molestation in general. Her mother went as far as taking her stepfather back when he got out of jail. Therefore, Jessica had a hard time trusting others, and she held hatred within her heart. Her hostility reached past her mother and stepfather, and affected all of those who were in direct contact with her. Jessica had a daughter of her own, and her mother constantly badgered her about seeing the girl. For reasons, which are completely understandable, Jessica kept her mother away from her daughter and did not want her to visit her mother, and even if she did, she would only allow her to see grand mom while she monitored the visit. She explained that the worst part is when her mother wanted Jessica to visit on holidays, and acted as if nothing happened between her and her stepfather. This infuriated her, and she felt as if her mother discredited her feelings, and chose her stepfather over her; and for that reason, she hated her.

Jessica was involved in a three-year relationship with her boyfriend but it was endangered because she refused to marry him, as she didn't trust him, and she did not allow him to build a relationship with her daughter. He threatened to leave her, and this put Jessica's emotions into overdrive. So when she heard me speak about forgiveness during my speech, something stirred inside of her, which had her reaching out to me to find more. In her email to me, she wanted to know how I found it in my heart to forgive the man who trafficked me, the man who abused me during our short-lived marriage, and the man who walked out on our children and never looked back. She said she didn't think she could ever be that strong to forgive her stepfather or mother. Jessica set an appointment with me and so began her path to forgiveness and freedom.

Some people afflicted with PTSD have pushed the pain of their trauma way down deep inside as a way to cope with the symptoms. They overcompensate in other areas of their lives such as Jessica has done over the years. Jessica was extremely successful. She was a corporate director, and she described herself as a no-nonsense employer who reveled when others called her a bitch (according to her words, not mine). She took delight in running a tight ship, and liked that she was the only woman in her division who oversaw around 75 employees. She boasted that she had a great work ethic, was trustworthy, and was the go-to person with an excellent memory. She stated she could recall the tiniest of details at her job. However, this wasn't so in her personal life. Jessica overcompensated in her professional life, because she felt she had no control over her personal life. She worked hard at being successful to prove to her family that she was worthy, and to make sure she would never have to lean on them for anything. Jessica divulged that she earned a college scholarship, graduated from High School, and left home at the age of 17.

After people have suffered trauma, they try to overcompensate in some ways in their lives in a bid to have a sense of importance. They also throw themselves into other aspects in their lives as a way to distance themselves from the trauma. When they do this, they often disassociate from what happened, and it is easy for them to forget specific details. Therefore, when Jessica came into my office for her life coaching appointment, she had a hard time trying to remember painful events of the past. She would often deflect and talk about other things. It was obvious that she was extremely uncomfortable with not being able to recall specific events that she actually falsified some of the story. She would apologize often, which I asked her not to do. It's not that Jessica intentionally tried to fabricate her story; it was due to the trauma she experienced. I find that when people experience trauma, they tend to create stories about their trauma, which is referred to a confabulation.

Confabulation is defined as made-up or fabricated memories about oneself, or the world that appear to be choppy, incomplete, or completely false. Understand that when some people confabulate their story, they are not purposely trying to do so. I like to attribute this to our brain trying to protect us from remembering things that hurt us. There are plenty of scientific arguments as to why our brains repress these memories. However, we *can* forget our traumatic events, but our brains do not erase the memories, only repress. For instance, although I have a vivid recollection of what happened to me during my time of being trafficked, it often comes in bits and pieces. There will be moments that I receive a rush of past information into my brain, and there are times when the memories come in fragments, and I am completely fine with that, trust me!

It is important to acknowledge the distressing or disturbing experience. In acknowledging that it happened, you are in fact accepting that something has happened. It's not always easy to do this. In doing so, you are essentially saying that you were hurt, you were not protected, or someone failed to protect you. You are acknowledging that you were vulnerable and someone took advantage of your vulnerability. This can bring up feelings that you had repressed for some time and make you feel quite uncomfortable. When Jessica started recollecting what her stepfather did to her, she encountered a wave of emotions that she hadn't experienced in a long time. At first, she wept uncontrollably, then became angry, wherein she swore her mother and stepfather. I asked that she allow all of her emotions come through in our safe place of meeting. When she was calm enough, we began working on the breathing techniques that I will explain to you later on in this book. From there, she was able to open up and talk about her painful memories, with much carefulness.

The discomfort of remembering keeps many people silent, and that silence represses the memory. If not careful, the bits and fragments can come back and cause mental impairment. It is okay to trust your memories, no matter how incredulous they sound. Often, when I am interviewed about my past, people want to get as specific as possible with the details to decipher if I am telling the truth or not. I can remember having brunch with someone who I thought was a friend. However, little did I know she was more interested in cross-examining me on the details of my trafficking story. It was quite strange the way she questioned me, and tried to read my body language, which brings me to the point of boundaries. You do not have to divulge any specifics of your past just to appease someone, especially since recollection of those memories can be triggers. I do not allow anyone to push my buttons, and cause me any emotional discomfort. I have set my boundaries so good that I have no problem telling an interviewer or person that they are pushing it, and stepping over their boundaries. We will go over boundary setting later on.

   Getting Jessica to open up and recall those events, which lay dormant in her mind, was no easy task. I saw the emotional turmoil, and finished our session with hands on Reiki to clear the blockages in her seventh chakras.

What memory is just too painful to remember that you just can't seem to forgive? Write it down so that you can visually see it.

I am holding on to the painful memory of:

_____

_____

_____

_____

_____

Now that you see it on paper, it becomes real, and you can better deal with this painful memory. The work to let go of this painful memory will become easier because you are being open and honest about it.

Chapter

6
Anger is a False Friend

"We must remember that anger is supposed to be only temporary. We must distance ourselves from anger because it has no place within our healing."

Do you remember when you were in grade or high school, and you familiarized yourself with anger? Do you remember when one of your close friends would become angry with someone, and they expected you to become angry with them, too? It was at that moment you allowed someone else to push his or her emotion onto you. Whether you felt that way or not, you agreed and went along with it, after all they were your friends; and if they were angry with someone, then you must take up this emotion and be angry too!

It could be that a family member projected their anger onto you and expected you to feel the same way. It happens often when a couple splits, and if the person who has the physical custody of the children is angry with the other parent or family, then watch out. That angry parent projects this hate and anger onto the children, and the poor kids are stuck with this heavy feeling without ever asking for it. It's seen on social media all of the time, one person posts something about being angry about a particular situation, all of a sudden, thousands of people jump on this bus headed down the angry highway. Some do it without even knowing the particulars of why they are supposedly angry. Next time you see this bandwagon effect, ask the people in question why they are angry and, usually they will have a hard time explaining it to you.

Anger is not a welcomed emotion that makes you feel good. In fact, anger is heavy and can stifle your spiritual growth. It's an easy emotion to settle into, it's warm and very inviting at the moment. It feels comfy at first, and oh so righteous because you finally have a way to describe how you feel about a particular person or situation. But don't get too comfortable with this emotion because anger is sneaky and not to be trusted. What feels like a welcomed emotion at first turns around and bites you just like a snake.

Anger begins to take over your life. It buries deep within you and starts to take root there. It won't allow any other emotion to take up space within you. It wants all of your attention. Pretty soon, it turns into hatred and low vibrations. Anger is demanding and too controlling. It turns into jealousy. Before you know it, you will start to become envious of others and you have no idea how it all started. It all started with the anger.

Anger likes to stay with you and justify itself by pointing out all of the things that are wrong within your life; it loves to play the blame game wherein you are the victim. Before long, you can't focus on the things that are going well with your life, and it takes away any inclination of gratitude that may be lingering within your mind. Anger turns into depression, sadness, guilt, and shame.

When I suffered from PTSD, my fear turned into anger and hatred. For instance, after being trafficked, I became angry with my mother; I reasoned she didn't protect me enough, and that she never protected me from the wrath of men. Anger took up space within my heart and every time I looked at her or spoke to her, I would make an argument and literally try to have a physical altercation with her. Imagine that, imagine me hating and trying to physically hurt the one person who brought me into the world, loved me, and nurtured me until I was able to do it on my own. My mother had no idea of where and how this hurt and anger originated. She thought perhaps I had started to take drugs. She had no idea that I was angry about the pain I endured due to being trafficked.

Deep down, I didn't want to hurt her. I actually wanted her to embrace, love, and protect me. I wanted her to promise the little girl that was inside of me that I wouldn't be hurt anymore; that she would make sure the bad guys would leave me alone, for good. Upon going to therapy, I realized that it was all misplaced anger and pain from the trauma. I was able to apologize and ask for forgiveness from the one person who loved me the most in the world.

When we suffer from trauma, anger becomes our friend along with the other low vibrational emotions—hurt, suffering, pain, depression, shame, and guilt. We must remember that anger is supposed to be only temporary. We must distance ourselves from anger because it has no place within our healing. It has no place within our lives for good; so we must ensure that we recognize this emotion, accept it, and finally release it. If you are angry, reflect on how long you have been angry. Then make a conscious decision to release it for good.

Here is a prayer to help you release your anger:

"Dear God, I ask that you help me to release the ties that bind me to anger. I ask that you replace anger with love and healing. I release all of my anger to you, because the burden is much too heavy for me to bear. Amen"

Chapter

7
Breathe Through It

"Sitting on my mat, I learned to acknowledge, embrace, and welcome my anxiety by asking it to continue and to increase if it wanted to. I had to learn how to trust my body all over again."

Did you know there was an art to breathing correctly? Think about it, most of us don't really pay attention to the way we breathe, the number of breaths we take, the quality of inhaling and exhaling. It is just happening without much of an effort on our part unless we have a medical condition. I would like to bring your awareness to breathing correctly. When I escaped my trauma of being trafficked, I would often suffer from anxiety attacks. Anxiety attacks are brought on by fear. It is when your body enters a mode of panic for no particular reason. Fear is your body's natural alarm that is meant to warn you that something isn't right, and you are being threatened. It also puts you in the "fight or flight" response, and it's an important element of human survival. When you are in the "fight or flight" mode, the amygdala gets overloaded and becomes hyper-vigilant. This is when you experience an anxiety attack.

After my torment, these attacks would come any time I had a trigger, or reminisced about my past. One particular time I was driving on the highway, and I started to reminisce about my painful ordeal and all of a sudden, my stomach felt queasy. Then I began to feel warm, and my heart began to pound fast and hard. I felt like I couldn't breathe, and I honestly thought I was going to die. I managed to pull over to the side of the highway, put the car in a park, and I tried to catch my breath. I started to feel lightheaded, and I managed to dial my mother on the phone. As best as I could, I explained to her what was happening and she talked me through it. She told me that I was okay, and that whatever was troubling me would pass. After I finally calmed down, I knew I had to gain control over my anxiety, or my anxiety would fully control me. I enrolled in a meditation class and that is where I learned the art of breathing.

When experiencing an anxiety attack sometimes you will feel the following symptoms: a sensation of upset or nausea in your stomach, muscle tension or shaking, dizziness, racing heartbeat, chest pain, flushing skin, and difficulty in breathing. Trust me when I say it can make you feel like you're going to pass out, lose your mind, or die.

In meditation, I was oriented in the correct way to breathe. The first thing I learned is that while having anxiety attacks, you hyperventilate. Hyperventilation is a condition whereby low carbon dioxide levels in the body eventually lead to the narrowing of the blood vessels that supply blood to the brain. It makes you feel lightheaded and dizzy, and you can actually pass out. Although there isn't a way to completely stop hyperventilating immediately when you are in a full anxiety mode, there are ways to prevent the symptoms from becoming worst. First thing to do is to try and slow down the breathing by taking a full 5 seconds to inhale, and exhale for 7 seconds. This sends oxygen to the brain, and your breathing will slow down on its own. The one thing I was surprised to learn was that I was wrong for trying to stop the panic attacks. I had to learn to allow the attacks to come, and even welcome them! In doing so, I honored my body and respected its right to try to keep me protected. My brain wasn't doing anything wrong, it knew we had been hurt, and in an effort to warn me from future danger, it was constantly on the lookout. I was paranoid as well. Sitting on my mat, I learned to acknowledge, embrace, and welcome my anxiety by asking it to continue and to increase if it wanted to. I had to learn how to trust my body all over again.

You see, what I learned is that after the suffering, I no longer trusted myself, or that I could keep myself safe. So even while in a place like a yoga center, seated on a mat, and surrounded by peaceful individuals, I started to, you guess it, suffer an anxiety attack. My body was scared and wanted me to grab my shoes and get the hell out of there. It didn't trust that I was safe. So the courteous small blonde yoga teacher, who was in the middle of the class, noticed that I was starting to have an attack, and she told the class to continue with their pose and walked right over to me. She took my hands gently, looked into my eyes, and started speaking softly to me, "You are safe. This is a safe place. No one will harm you here. You are loved. It's alright."

She smiled sweetly, and I mimicked her small lips, "Inhale, 1, 2, 3, 4, 5, good. Now exhale, 1, 2, 3, 4, 5, 6, 7." She further coaxed me along.

"Let me hear your breath on the exhale, force it out loud."

I was surprised to see the other students had joined in on the breathing as well. After ten breathing counts of 5, she just walked back to the front of the room and took up where she left off. Embarrassed, I busied myself with the remainder of the poses. She never asked me why I had the anxiety attacks, and I never told her.

Meditation helped me because it calmed my emotions down and rewired my brain. Mediation has been shown to improve emotional regulation by decreasing the hyperactivity of amygdala.

A prayer for you if you experience anxiety:

"Dear God, I ask that you help me to be kinder and gentler with myself. Help me to trust my body. Help me to breathe through it all and heal from my anxiety. Amen."

Chapter

8
Affirmations & Mantras

I am a firm believer in affirmations and mantras. I also used mantras to heal my anxiety. The word mantra is a Sanskrit word. A mantra is a word, sound, formula, or incantation of prayer repeated to aid in concentration. So, while breathing in, I would say *I am calm*; and while breathing out, I said, *I am safe*. I said this for the duration of my meditations twice a day for well over a year. While that might sound like a long time for some, let's just say, I haven't had a panic attack in over 12 years!

My client Leslie came to me at 16 years old and during her time of receiving professional help from me, it was revealed that her mother called her damaging names, and told her repeatedly that she would never amount to anything. She could remember being told this from the time she was around 8 or 9 years old. Leslie had no self-esteem and she never had any good things to say about herself. She had no plans for the future, as she couldn't even see herself graduating from high school. Leslie had a shortsighted future, and told me there was nothing good about her life.

Affirmations are important in instances like Leslie's because while you are saying them, you are recording them subconsciously in your brain. Affirmations help to change your tape. What we think replays in our minds over and over like a looped tape. If we were consistently slammed with negative talk throughout childhood and young adulthood, we would grow up with awful thought pattern. Negative thoughts would have become programmed in our brains. Nonetheless, negative thought patterns can be broken with affirmations. We can rewrite our thoughts with positive ones, which will boost our self-esteem and give us self-worth and a positive outlook on life.

I helped Leslie to change her tape with the following affirmations:

- I am a unique, beautiful, and smart person.
- The Creator gave me rare gifts to share with this world.
- I am worthy of good things.
- I love, appreciate, and approve of myself.
- I accept my past, and look forward to my bright future.
- I replace my anger with compassion.
- I trust myself to make decisions that are right for me.
- I surround myself with positive and kind people.
- It doesn't matter what anyone else thinks of me, I love myself.
- I am grateful every day.

I provide my own children with affirmations, which have been a wonderful foundation for forgiveness and a great self-esteem boost. I have personally recorded affirmations for trauma survivors, and a specific set of affirmations to practice forgiveness and invoke healing. It's important to repeat affirmations at least twice a day to help change your tape; once in the morning when you wake, and before you retire to bed at the night time. If you really want to change your thinking, try listening to audio affirmation recordings while you are sleeping by going to my site, the *greenlightofforgiveness.com.*

Chapter

9

You Want Me to Do What?

My client Belinda reached out to me via social network, and asked if I could make contact with her deceased son, and since I perform medium work, I agreed to do it. However, on the day she came for her session, my spirit told me that I needed to help heal her mental anguish first before attempting to make contact with her son. I had worked with her three times in conjunction with the clinical therapy she was receiving. In each session, understandably she broke down to the point where we couldn't continue. She blamed herself for her son's murder. It isn't uncommon for people to blame themselves when they had absolutely nothing to do with their trauma. Still she found a way to include herself, going as far as telling me that if she had listened to the voice of her intuition and made him stay home instead of letting him visit a friend, he would still be alive.

Belinda suffered from PTSD symptoms that ranged from her reliving the incident as she imagined it, to sleeplessness, irritability, and clinical depression. Belinda also suffered from suicidal ideation. She was on prescription sedatives that she loathed, and wanted to stop taking them. When I asked Belinda if she thought she would be able to forgive the young man who murdered her son, she looked at me with her eyes widened, leaned in, and said, "Why would I? He ruined my life!"

I leaned in toward her and said, "I understand your pain, but your hatred is making you physically ill. I think at some point when you're ready, you will need to forgive him."

Belinda threw both of her hands up in exasperation, shook her head in disbelief, and said, "You want me to do what now?"

I sat upright, looked into her eyes, and repeated myself. I knew this session would prove difficult because she was in no way prepared to forgive the man who took her first born away from her; and as the mother of a son, I couldn't blame her. So it came as no surprise that at the very mention of forgiving her son's murderer, she had a full on panic attack.

Belinda stated that her sons' killer didn't seem to have an ounce of remorse for what he'd done at first, but after he was sentenced, he read a prepared statement where he talked about his negative and dangerous background. Without wanting too, she empathized where his callous nature and attitude came from. She expressed that the guilt and anger was consuming her; so much so, that she wasn't any good to her other children. She was filled with so much grief that they were basically on their own. She and her husband hadn't had sexual intercourse since her son's death, and she feared that they were drifting apart. She spent her time in her son's room, at church, sitting off to herself, or lying in bed. Belinda was exhausted, and it was registered all over her face. Her body was riddled with pain from muscle soreness and tightness. She complained of her heart hurting, and feared she would have a heart attack. It was obvious her heart chakra was completely blocked, and it needed clearing.

I asked Belinda to journal about the idea of forgiveness and share her journal entry with me on our next meeting. The following week, Belinda read her entry to me and I was surprised and relieved. She expressed how the pain of guilt and anger was almost as unbearable as not being able to see her son again. She stated that it was tearing her up inside, and tearing her family apart. She went on to say that she wanted to forgive the young man but didn't know where to start. She also admitted that she was afraid to forgive him, afraid of what it would feel like to allow the words, "I forgive you," roll off her tongue. She said that she discussed it over with her clinician and that the clinician was pretty much in agreement with me, that to forgive would start a new chapter in her grieving process. With a small smile, and hope in her eyes, Belinda was finally ready to begin the *Green Light of Forgiveness* process.

A prayer to open up to the idea of forgiveness:

"Dear God, please help me to open up my mind, and accept the things I cannot change, and to change my way of thinking so that I can open to the idea of forgiveness. Help me to forgive as you do. Amen."

Chapter

10
Exactly What is Forgiveness?

To forgive someone, you have to know exactly what it means. Dictionary.com defines it as, *to grant pardon for or remission; absolve*. I, for one, don't necessarily believe this definition fits within every scenario. There are simply some acts that are rather hard to *pardon*. I believe the definition, *to cease to feel resentment against* is much more aligned with the art of forgiving someone within the context of this book. For the mother who lost her son, would she grant a pardon to the person who took his life? Perhaps. But is it wrong of her to want the person who took her son's life to pay for their crime? Ultimately, she will want to cease feeling resentful toward this person, so that she can have peace and be able to go on with her life.

Simply put, it is up to the person to decide upon which acts they are willing to pardon, and excuse. But eventually, we all must find it within our hearts to cease feeling resentment so we can feel at peace. For instance, as for the wife who excuses her husband for having an extramarital affair, she can find peace in her marriage if she stops feeling resentment toward him. Consider my client who suffered from sexual abuse at the hand of her stepfather; no, she would not excuse, nor pardon his act. She, however, wants to let go of the extreme hatred and resentment, which she is slowly doing with time. It is totally dependent on the situation but you can choose in which context you want to forgive someone.

Think back to when you learned about forgiveness, who taught you? What did forgiveness look like for you? I learned about forgiveness early on in my life with the complex, yet simple relationship between my parents. They had a long history together, and although everything is calm now, it wasn't always this way. So as a young girl, I learned that there was pain involved with forgiveness, and that the pain could be heavy. And although you might not have been ready to do so, you still forgave that person and moved forward. I continued that very pattern in my own romantic relationships.

My intimate relationships with men were rocky back then, there really isn't anything more to say about that. I had to break the pattern that I was born into, the pattern that I learned from early childhood. You know the expression, *when you know better you do better*? This is true. Once I realized that love did not have to equal pain, suffering, or misery, I changed it up real quick! I had to forgive my mother for not teaching me better by her actions; after all, she is human and, of course, a byproduct of what she had been taught. Then I had to forgive myself for not knowing the difference, and just repeating a behavioral pattern.

Forgiveness should be on your terms, not the person that performed the bad behavior, or the person who caused the pain. No one can bully you into forgiving him or her. Abusers like to do this. How? Within the cycle of domestic violence, you will often find the abusers demanding their victims to take them back, or coerce the victims to take them back. They insist the victim is to blame for their own abuse and the abusers' ways. So the victim starts to feel guilty and actually forgives them whether they are ready to or not. Remember this, no one deserves abuse on any level; and most certainly, you are not to blame for someone abusing you. You are not on anyone's clock to forgive him or her. It is fine to take your time and work on forgiving others. The important part is that you consider it.

Again, you do not have to forgive anyone's actions but it is wise to face, accept what happened, and eventually have the courage to let it go. If you refuse to forgive someone, you are essentially saying, "I want to hold on to this pain, misery, and suffering inside of me. Not because it feels good, but because I feel safe in this place of despair, at this dead end. I want you to always remember how badly you hurt me and in doing so, you will hurt because I hurt. I *need* you to feel hurt the way you have hurt me."

Let me let you in on this little secret, you are not hurting the person who hurt you by not forgiving them! They will never truly hurt the way they hurt you. Your feelings are just that, your feelings. Forgiveness is not about them, but all about you. Forgiving them has no bearing on them one way or the other. When you forgive, you release. You let go of all that pain, suffering, and trauma. You will always remember what happened to you, but it will no longer affect you in the ways that unforgiveness does now. By not practicing forgiveness, you are still giving that other person control. By virtue of unforgiveness, they control how you feel (with suffering), how you think (with negative thoughts continuously about them), with how you act (if you are acting in any way, which is not for your highest good). So by practicing forgiveness, you are taking your power back. You control how you feel, think, and act. You do so by doing what is best for your highest good.

Is love involved with forgiveness? You might not want to hear this but yes, it is. Love is involved with forgiveness; but not the type of emotional, feeling-based love that you are equating it with. You practice **agape** love with forgiveness.

Agape Love

First let me tell you that there are different forms of love! The New Testament of the Holy Bible was written in Koine Greek. During this time, there were several words, which explained different kinds of love. There was *eros* (erotic), which was all about sexual love; *storge*, or *astorgous* the type of love you have for family; *philia*, which is heartfelt, genuine love. You might have this type of love for a best friend. The noblest love of them all is *agape*. This type of love has nothing to do with affection, the emotions; it does not come from your heart. Agape love comes from your mind. It's the kind of love that we should have for humankind. In my groups, I often tell the participants that they are loved, that I love them. They usually look at me as if I am crazy, and say, "But you don't even know us, how can you love us?" That's when I explain that I love humankind, and I have love for humanity. I follow the scripture Matthew 5:44 in the Holy Bible. It reads that we must have agape love for all humankind, even our enemies. Let me be clear, before I became a believer of Jesus Christ, I still believed that we must have agape love. I didn't even know what agape love was, nor did I know it was listed in the Bible. Deep down in my heart, I felt this to be true; I resonated deep within my soul to have love for humankind.

If this is your first time hearing of this, you might want to close this book and throw it across the room in protest of what I'm saying. If you don't believe in the Bible, then you might not think this applies to you. But I want you to think about this for a moment. Even if you aren't a Christian, or you don't believe in the Holy Bible, I want you to think about how you feel about certain things. These include, but not limited to, the following:

- Do you care about our environment?
- Do you care about animals?
- Do you care about the suffering of man in Third World countries, or war-torn countries?
- Do you care about children who suffer at the hands of abusers?
- Do you ever give money to charities, the homeless?
- Do you ever go out of your way to do an act of kindness?

If you said yes to any of the questions above, then you do love, with the agape style.

Chapter

11
When It's Too Late

There may be a time when you want to ask for forgiveness from someone, or forgive a situation with people who refuse to speak to you again, or who have passed over into the spirit world. I want you to know that it's all right. I want you to know that you can still use *The Green Light of Forgiveness,* when faced with this situation. Let me give you an example.

I had a 14-year-old client named Tiffany who struggled with being obedient and listening to her mother. Her mother suffered from health conditions that made her wheelchair bound, and unable to get around as much as she'd like. This angered Tiffany who was a teenager as she longed to have a mother-and-daughter relationship with her mother like any other *normal* teenagers (whatever normal is in her view). She often lamented how her mother was cripple, lame, and down right embarrassing. So Tiffany acted out in ways unimaginable for a girl her age. She became a habitual runaway, started experimenting with drugs, and stopped going to school altogether. Each time Tiffany was apprehended by authorities, and taken to Juvenile, her mother's health would decline, and she would have to be hospitalized for an extended period. When Tiffany would hear of her mother's hospitalization, she would appear indifferent. She would just shrug and say, "I don't care!"

The last time Tiffany ran away, her mother went back into the hospital for another extended period. I spoke with her mother, and this woman shared how much she loved her daughter, and it was her wish that she would find her way, and just be the good girl she remembered when she was younger. I usually went to visit Tiffany's mother whenever she was in the hospital, but this particular time, I had a vacation planned, for which I was on my way to my chosen destination, the next day. Instead of going to see her like my first mind told me, I boarded a flight to Mexico for some much-needed relaxation and rest. I told myself that the Tiffany fiasco would work itself out like it usually does, and that I would attend to it when I got back.

As soon as I touched down in Mexico, I got to the resort, put my bags down in my room, and headed to the beach. I took my shoes off and walked alongside the shore allowing the sand to kiss my feet. The tide tickled my ankles, as I gazed out toward the sun. It was very calm, and I was amused that I had the beach pretty much to myself at that time of day. Then all of a sudden, a huge gush of wind enveloped me and almost knocked me off my feet. I felt a sort of warmth come over me, and I immediately thought of Tiffany's mother. I stated out loud, "It's okay, Ms. Jones, I love you, too," and I hugged my arms and continued to walk down the beach. I found a beautiful bolder where I chose to do some quick meditation. I enjoyed that week long vacation, and when I got back to Las Vegas, I called to check in with my employees. I got some shocking news that Ms. Jones passed away the very day I left for Mexico.

I was taken aback, and stunned. I thought I had plenty of time; I thought I was going to come back and go the hospital to see her. But what perplexed me most was I instantly knew that the gush of wind I felt on the beach, the moment I talked to her out loud, I was saying my last goodbye. Ms. Jone's spirit found me in Mexico, to let me know that it would be okay, and that she loved me! She always told me how much she loved me for trying to help her daughter and her family. She always expressed how much she appreciated me. I initially felt guilty for putting aside my initial thought of not going to see her before I left, but quickly got over it when I realized we had our moment in Mexico.

Tiffany did not have the same kind of luck. Unfortunately, she was in Juvenile Detention the moment her mother crossed over into the spirit world. Upon her being told her mother died, she took it hard, and never fully recovered. Tiffany got out of detention and went into a mental institution by her own asking. She felt tremendous guilt for her mother's demise, though it wasn't her fault. She couldn't come to terms that she would never be able to say goodbye to her mother, or make things right.

Perhaps when Tiffany is older, she will come to term with her mothers' death. But this is an example of when you think it's too late.

Maybe the person(s) you desire forgiveness from is still living but unwilling to hear you out. Maybe you've done something you think is so deplorable that there's no making it right. You can always be forgiven if it is coming from your heart. You do not need the other person's blessing to be forgiven. You only need to ask the Creator to forgive you first, and then you will have to forgive yourself. Below is a prayer for you to ask the Creator for forgiveness, and then in the next chapter, I will teach you how to forgive yourself with *The Green Light of Forgiveness Meditation.*

"Creator I ask you to please have mercy on me, and to forgive me for what I have done to _____(fill in their names), for _____(fill in the blank). I know through your grace and mercy you have forgiven me. Amen."

Chapter

12
The Green Light of Forgiveness Meditation

"Remember, God is love. He isn't half love, or conditional love. He is complete agape love. In order for you to truly be able to practice forgiveness and move on, it is necessary for you to try and love."

We're finally here, the point of this book, The Green Light of Forgiveness. The idea of forgiving someone seems as if we are giving him or her all of our power, and making ourselves appear weak. This is actually untrue. It takes bravery, courage, and patience to forgive others when they cause us great pain, but in doing so, we take our power back. We are taking control over our own emotions. Can you imagine a world where everyone energetically held on to every single negative thing that someone did to him or her, no matter how great or small? Actually, it appears as if that is happening in our world today because so many people are walking around angry and upset, with chips on their shoulders. People are blaming others, the government, religion, and even nature for their problems. What we see is the absence of compassion. We must have compassion for the environment, animals, people, and, most of all, ourselves.

Compassion is the ability to sympathize and suffer with another person's suffering. When we lack compassion, we carry an, *I don't care* attitude. This leads to selfishness and a blatant disregard for humanity. A majority of my clients are surprised to learn that they must first have compassion for themselves, which leads them to forgiving themselves.

Forgiving ourselves is no easy task. To forgive ourselves would mean that we have to first admit that something has happened to us, or that we have witnessed something so disturbing that it has disrupted our daily living pattern. We sometimes hold ourselves to a greater standard than we do others. We tell ourselves that we should have done more, been more, and known better. We go on to think that we somehow allowed the unfortunate incident to happen. When we think like this, we are being hard on ourselves, and not coming from a loving place. In most instances, people are quick to forgive others before they can even fathom to forgive themselves. In Belinda's session, she was extremely hard on herself, as she actually blamed herself for her son's unfortunate early demise. She took full responsibility for what the other person did. She had a very hard time letting go of the notion that she should have, and possibly could have done more to keep her son alive. Thinking this way made Belinda take on physical illness—she suffered from frequent headaches and stomach pains. She had to admit that thinking this way was exhausting and dangerous. It was dangerous because of the implications this had on her physical and mental health. Remember, she had suicidal ideation as well, with thoughts that she no longer wanted to live due to the guilt and extreme grief she had. She said the only reason she was still living is because her other children needed her.

With Belinda unable to forgive herself for what she think she did or did not do, this thought pattern kept her in a victimization state, and unable to move forward.

The Why?

In order to forgive yourself, you need to know exactly what you are forgiving yourself for. You need to examine the memories, feelings, and situations, for which you're seeking forgiveness. Ask yourself the following questions:
1. Am I feeling this way about an outcome because of something I personally did?
2. Am I feeling this way about an outcome because of what someone else did?

If you are personally to blame for an outcome due to something you have done, then you need to accept that bad things happen to everyone; that due to your actions, there was a failure. You also need to understand that failure happens to everyone. You will achieve a varying degree of different failures throughout your life. Failure is necessary, and teaches us a lesson. However, with failure, you have to learn how to *fail up*, how to *get good at failing*.

When you get good at failing, or fail up, you acknowledge that you've failed and you learned a lesson from it. Good failure will teach a life lesson that you can apply to daily living. It is something that you can teach others. For example, for many years, I blamed myself for being trafficked. I would beat myself up with the thought that if I hadn't gone out by myself, or agreed to meet my trafficker for breakfast, I wouldn't have been in that situation. However, I accepted that it happened; I am grateful that I survived, and now I am a public speaker on the subject of sex trafficking. I travel all over the country, speaking mainly at universities where I educate on the topic of trafficking, give tips on how to stay safe, and what to do in case of trafficking. In this way, I have failed up, I failed up because I am using my trauma for good; I took back my power by using my voice, telling my story, and educating people along the way.

I realized that I did not cause the pain due to the outcome of my experience of being trafficked. My trafficker was the person who caused the pain and the emotions after the outcome. Therefore, I accepted that it was not my fault. I struggled with the notion that I wasn't to blame for placing myself in that situation, but I had to realize that no one is perfect, and that it doesn't matter that I went out by myself or that I met with someone for food and conversation. There is never a point where taking another person's freedom, or threating them with physical harm or death, is ever appropriate. I had to extend compassion toward myself, and be gentle with myself. Although I knew it wasn't entirely my fault that I was trafficked, I still forgave myself because I was a little hard on myself, calling myself stupid for even accepting his offer to join him at the restaurant. I know what it's like to beat and torture yourself mentally.

    I had a client, Kathy who came to me as a survivor of sexual trauma. Needless to say, she had a lot of forgiving to do. She suffered from sexual molestation as a child and at the age of 16, she had enough and finally ran away. But the abuse had really just begun while she was homeless. She met the wrong person and became trafficked, physically abused, and addicted to methamphetamines. Years later, although she no longer was in the situation, she suffered heavily from PTSD. As a way to relieve the emotional pain, she began to injure herself. Kathy practiced self-mutilation and as a cutter, she had large perforated skin lesions from the areas on her wrists where she cut regularly. Kathy stated it felt good to cut herself, and it gave her a sense of relief when she saw the blood. No matter what the situation, she blamed herself for everything. She never had one good thing to say about herself, and she talked down to herself all of the time. Although she cut herself regularly in an effort to have some type of control over her own body, she still felt helpless in the deepest part of her being. When I met her, I helped her understand why forgiveness was at the center of it all if she were to ever find relief. I taught her the *Green Light of Forgiveness* meditation to aid in the healing process.

Green Light of Forgiveness Meditation

In order to perform this meditation, it is important that you have done required 'pre-work' to either rid yourself of PTSD symptoms, or have them under control with the help of your clinician. If you have not worked on your trauma symptoms and you are still suffering, please stop reading this book now before proceeding. If you are, let's proceed. You can also gain some insight through my personally recorded YouTube video at the G*reenLightofForgiveness.com.*

First, you will need to make sure that you are in a safe place where there are no triggers. A place where you feel supported and secure will be a great meditation spot. Ensure that there are no distractions such as chatter, television, music, or the disturbance of your telephone. Make sure you have a white candle (and soft meditation music if you desire). Wear comfortable clothing that will make you feel relaxed. Light up your candle, and if handy, place a couple of drops of essential oils onto your skin, or inhale them to help you to relax. Let's move on to the actual meditation.

Make sure your root chakra and feet are grounded onto the floor. You can do this by either lying down on your back or sitting; whichever is comfortable. Begin by taking five deep mindful breaths to release any tension that you might be feeling in your body. Remember to breathe in through the nose by taking in a full five seconds to inhale, and exhale through the mouth for seven seconds. When you exhale, make sure you are making a sound. The point is to hear your breath on the exhale, force it out loudly. Try and relax each part of your body while keeping your mind alert. Once you feel relaxed, it is time to begin the meditation.

You can meditate with your eyes open as you focus on the flickering flame of the candle or you can choose a place in the distance to focus on. If you decide to keep your eyes closed, this is fine too. Think of your heart chakra and picture a soft green light illuminating from your chest. The first thing you need to do is bathe yourself in this green light. Imagine the soft green light covering you from head to toe. Watch this light pierce through your body, and permeate every place on your body. Place your hand over your heart and say the following:

(State your name), "_____I apologize, I love you, and I forgive you for _____."

(State your name), "_____ I honor you, I respect you, and you are safe."

Repeat these affirmations until you forgive everything that you blame yourself for. It's important to apologize to yourself not only because you put yourself through so much mental turmoil of shame, blame, and guilt; but also because, at some level, you may have actually had a small part in whatever you blamed yourself for, and that is alright. No one is perfect, and you must practice the same compassion the Creator extends to you. There isn't anything that you can't ask forgiveness for. Remember we are all human and the Creator forgives, and so should you. It's hard to accept the fact that no matter how bad something was at some point in our lives, no matter how much the pain hurt, we were an actual vibrational match for this pain. Sounds weird, right? See, we operate on a vibrational level. When I was still rather worldly and hadn't accepted my spiritual gifts I was stuck at a low vibrational level. I identified with the *'woe is me'* mentality, always saying how much my life sucked, and declared that bad things were always happening to me. Things did! I stayed in drama-filled mess and bad relationships; jobs sucked; I always received speeding tickets, and my credit sucked. I was rarely happy.

I am not saying that people who suffer trauma are all on low vibrations. Let's face it, awful things happen to good people even when they operate on a high vibration—it's just a part of life. The difference is that people who operate on a high vibrational level tend to understand that they are a spiritual being, but having a human experience. In this life, you will have pain, and pain is an awakening of sorts to remind you of this human condition, to remind us that we will all suffer at one point or another, and it's not actually about the suffering but how you respond to the suffering. How you choose to live your life from this moment on matters. It's important to note that when you survive trauma, it's how you use your story, give back, and help someone else who might be suffering now from what you've gone through. In order to give your pain some good purpose, you have to forgive those who have hurt you. Let's move forward so I can show you how.

Since the color green is associated with the heart chakra. It only seems appropriate that we should bathe the person who has hurt us in this space, in this soft color of green, which is still surrounding our body. This beautiful purifying color is also associated with nature, peace, and harmony. Green brings psychological and emotional harmony and balance. Take your five deep breaths, relax your body, and with your eyes focused or closed, imagine the person you need to forgive floating above you with their legs shoulder-width apart, arms stretched out, and slowly rotating. While they are rotating, imagine the soft green light being projected from your heart chakra toward them with the intention of forgiveness. Bathe them in this light; permeate every part of their body, mind, and soul with this beautiful green light. Pierce their heart center with a strong green laser light. Cleanse them in this light, and only operate from your heart chakra. When you see this person, do not see them with your earthly eyes, mind, or emotions. You are purely operating from the heart chakra. Now when you feel they are completely engulfed in your green light of forgiveness, say aloud or to yourself:

> (State their name), "_____I forgive you for _____, I apologize, and I love you."
>
> "I choose to let this situation go so that I may live freely."

Why are we saying we love this person or thing that has caused us pain? Remember, God is love. He isn't half love, or conditional love. He is complete agape love. In order for you to truly be able to practice forgiveness and move on, it is necessary for you to try and love—not the love that comes from the heart, but the kind of love that God has for us. It's the love that comes from the mind; it is not from the heart. When I tell people that I forgive and love the person who has traumatized me, they look at me crazy and tell me that something is probably wrong with me. I assure you there is nothing wrong with me. When you forgive and declare love for the person who caused you pain, you are not saying you are in love with them nor tolerate what they have done to you. No, you are saying you love them the way God loves them. You are not operating from your heart, emotions, or your feelings. It is the love that we are supposed to have for others as the result of the love we have for God. There are no strings attached; nothing is expected from it. We all have something called free will.

You're probably freaking out about having to apologize for the person who wronged you! I understand, don't go cursing me out or flinging the book across the bed. You are neither apologizing for anything that they have done, nor anything that you have supposedly done. You are simply apologizing that you were a vibrational match at the time. You are simply saying I'm sorry.

Don't dwell on the aspect of having to love your enemy too much because if you do, you will operate from the EGO, and your feelings. You are to forgive from your heart, but love from your mind. I can't express the importance of forgiving enough but trust me, if you don't forgive you will be stuck, unhappy, pretending to be okay, and mentally replaying the tape of your trauma over and over. It took me forever to say "I apologize; I love you" about all the people who wronged and hurt me. Still I did it, and what has emerged from that is a beautiful life, a peaceful soul, and a wonderful space. I didn't pick up a phone to call anyone to say the words, nor did I do it in front of them. I simply practiced the Green Light of Forgiveness meditation, and my energy aligned with the universe and I was elevated to a couple of levels.

I was briefly involved in a relationship with a man who lied to me for the entire time we were together. He swore that he was faithful, but as it turned out, he was involved in a full two-year relationship with another woman. I had to forgive him in order to have inner peace. I had to forgive myself first because I ignored my inner voice that told me repeatedly that he wasn't the one for me. I had to forgive myself for accepting someone I really wasn't a vibrational match for. I stayed in that relationship in an effort not to be alone. I forgave myself for not listening to my inner voice, and subjecting myself to someone who had no integrity. I forgave myself for not wanting to be alone and being in a relationship out of desperation. In order to move forward and have inner peace, the affirmation of love, apology, and forgiveness has to happen. There is no other way around it. I wish there were, but there isn't.

So, repeat as many times as necessary for you to accept this affirmation and actually hold it true. Once you have stated everything you forgive them for, it is time to move on to the next person or actual situation. That's right, *situation* because sometimes we are angry with the government, the military, corporations, jobs, religious organizations, etc. There is no limit to whom or what you can forgive. Also, you can do it as often as needed until you feel you have cleared the negativity and drama for good. Trust me, I have had to practice the *Green Light of Forgiveness* on certain people about twenty times, but each time, it gets easier and easier. The point here is that you have a tool with this meditation to get some closure even when the person or thing hasn't given you the closure that you desire. You don't need closure from them because you can get it for yourself. You don't need permission from anyone to move on. You can move on without their apologies, explanations, sympathy, or empathy. You can do this because you are meeting their spirit on a soul level. The person who refuses to take responsibility or apologize is operating out of ego, and they are oblivious to their spirits. So you are meeting them and forgiving them at their core without them even realizing it.

Many people come to me angry because the person who caused them pain won't express remorse for what they have done, and this pisses them off. Remember, the only thing that matters is that you take your power back by exercising forgiveness, so you can elevate yourself onto the next level. When you forgive, you move up the elevation ladder, and the person who feels as if they have nothing to apologize for remains right where they are on a low vibration. It's not your concern what they think of you, or how they feel about you, or even if they're sorry for what they've done; because honestly you can't make someone feel sorry for what they've done. Again, it's not your problem. The only concern you have is leaving the situation behind, elevating, and moving on to a higher vibration.

A prayer for forgiving and moving forward:

"God, thank you for the strength and courage that's necessary to forgive. Please, help me to accept what has happened, and give me the support to continue my healing. I will give this situation to you, let this go, and walk in your light going forward. Amen."

Chapter

13
Cut the Attachments

It is necessary to cut the attachments that you have with some of the people you had to forgive. Chord cutting can be easily done, and it does not have to involve some grand ceremony. When you come into contact with a person, you can immediately tell their aura, or their energy field. You know if they reside on a low or high vibration. What you probably didn't realize is that the people you interact with share energy with you, which is why you think of them from time to time, and wonder where they are, or what they are doing. When we sever ties with people we want to, we simply cut them off. Cord cutting is essentially the same thing.

The energy field or our 'aura' is different for every person and it can extend from anywhere from a few inches, to a hundred feet or more! When people describe me, they always talk about how my energy fills up the room. I know this to be true because my energy extends very far. I purposely extend my energy this far to cover the hundreds of angels that I have around me at all times. This energy covers our entire body, up, down; front to back, and side to side. This energy contains all of our personal information, everything about us;

it talks about our past lives, and reaches way beyond our future. Auras are constantly around us, and the people we have had interaction with as well.

Therefore, you'll want to cut the energy of the person you have forgiven off. Their energy is connected to you via a cord. Not a cable cord or anything, but an energy cord, and it can extend into the spiritual realm if that person is no longer physically with us! So I want you to think about this for a moment, if you have never cut cords, you have all of these cords attached to your aura, weighing you down, and dragging about you with their energy still co-mingling with yours. If you have ever thought about or done the following, yep that person still has a cord connected to you:

1. Thoughts about the person out of the blue
2. Thoughts about the person and you immediately became emotional (e.g. upset, or sad)
3. Dreams about a person
4. Thoughts of someone, and they instantly called or texted you.
5. Obsession with an altercation you had between you and another person

If you answered yes to any of these questions, we will need to do a cord cutting meditation to rid ourselves of these cords, to really let that person go once and for all. Now, if you answered yes to some of these questions but you are in a pleasant relationship with this person, then you might want to leave the cord intact. For instance, I have cords with my children, and immediate family. I never want to cut those cords, as they are beneficial and transfer a loving energy to me, which I adore. In this case, I want to keep these cords. On the flip side, if you are experiencing emotions or feelings of emotional upset, which prevent you from living the kind of life you deserve, it's time to cut those cords. If these feelings hinder your growth, or make you feel stagnant, then it's time to cut that cord. For instance, before I got divorced from my ex-husband, I was emotionally drained, upset, and completely unhappy. I was physically tired, and lived in a confused state. I had no idea how I ran my non-profit, worked a full-time job, and raised my two children. I had these cords well after we got divorced, when I started to live on my own. I made a decision to quit the relationship for good, mentally as well as physically, which required me to cut the cord. Amazingly enough, I didn't cut those cords until a year after leaving the marriage! They were some heavy cords! I needed assistance in cutting these cords and sought out an energy healer who was experienced in this area. So, if you feel you can't cut the cords alone, you can always seek out an energy healer to help you do so.

Cord Cutting Meditation

Acknowledge

The first thing we want to do before we meditate and cut the cords is to acknowledge whom we have these cords with. You will need to be honest with yourself in this instance, but it shouldn't be too hard because you have already forgiven them.

Identify

Then we come to the time to get in our meditative position by grounding our root chakra with the earth. Sit in a comfortable position, with your palms facing up resting lightly on your knees. Take your five deep mindful breaths. Close your eyes and identify the cords that are attached to your body. You will need to incorporate visualization here. The cords may differ in size, weight, and color depending on the person who attached them to you. You can pick these cords up and look at them, but remain calm. You may be surprised at how many you actually have. Do you know the expression, "This person is literally sucking the life out of me," or "This person really drains me!" They are, literally! They have cords attached to you doing so. Now, you acknowledge whom these cords are attached to, you see the cords, and you can move forward and cut them. Remember, if you see a cord attached to a person you lovingly accept in your aura, you may keep it. Just be careful not to disturb it, or accidently cut the wrong ones. With visualization, you should be fine.

Cut!

Now the fun part, cutting! You can use whatever method is right for you. If you visualize a pair of ceremonial scissors that you want to use to cut these cords, that is fine. Perhaps you want to get creative and use some sort of sword (I get it, Archangel Michael cuts my cords with his sword), or you might simply just want to use your bare hands to rip it out. Whatever you choose is fine. Visualize this cord and the other person on the other end of the cord, then pick the cord with your hands and proceed to cutting it from your end. You can do this in one clean swoop, or by pulling out string by string! Just note that is a long process, but if that is what you need to do to ensure that cord is cut, unraveled, and long gone by all means, have it. Just make sure you have set your intention to remove this cord, and all of its remnants and throw that end away from your energy field as far as you can see it. Once you have cut the final cord of the final person, you should feel much lighter, as you raised your vibration.

Afterward, make sure to wash your hands thoroughly and completely. I want to ensure you understand that once that cord is cut, that other person will know it has happened. They won't understand what actually happened, but they will know there has been a change in the relationship. They might try to reach out to you, or be in your energy field. This is not necessary, nor advised. You do not have to answer their texts or calls with, "I just cut your cord, honey. I don't mess with you!" No, do not engage in such a low vibrational conversation. No explanation needed. You do not have to have any type of exchange at all. But if you do interact with them, they will reattach this cord, and you will need to cut this cord all over again! It's best to send them the loving, healing green energy from your heart chakra just like in the *Green Light of Forgiveness* meditation.

The hard part is done, you have cut the cord, and it's time to move on to set some boundaries.

Chapter 14
Boundaries

"Remember, set boundaries that are on your terms, and at your own level of comfort. You do not owe anyone anything."

It's important to note that just because you forgive someone doesn't mean that you have to allow him or her into your space, or have access to you. Quite the contrary! Once you've done the hard work of forgiving them, it's time to be free to move on with or without them. There was a man who was wrongly accused of rape by a woman, and after serving many years in jail, he was acquitted, and released from prison. He and the woman, who accused him of this heinous crime, are close friends today. Try wrapping your head around that! Someone took your freedom and you become bosom buddies with them. This is the power of forgiveness! You don't have to be like this guy and get all chummy with people who have hurt you. For me, I practice forgiveness and move on. I don't linger in that same space with someone who has brought me unhappiness. The only exception I've made is with my father.

My father is a Vietnam Army veteran. He suffers from mental illness, dementia, and is 100% disabled. He has full mobility, but mentally he suffers. My family is the quintessential definition of forgiveness. While growing up, I witnessed my father being abusive toward my mother. He was equally verbally abusive as well. He would turn his words toward me, and those words physically hurt my heart. We endured so much at his hand within my family, and I ran to enlist in the military just to get away. I didn't run very far, as my father suffered from PTSD and reenacted for the Vietnam War. He hid in the bushes and committed a horrid act by shooting my brother in his leg with a BB gun due to a psychotic episode. I was serving in the military, and was stationed in Biloxi, Mississippi, when I received a call that my father was at the base gate in search of me. I didn't know at the time that he had shot my brother. Of course, I went to get him, and it wasn't until I picked him up and brought him home did I find out what happened. Confused, grief stricken, and embarrassed, I was dumbfounded and hurt. Thankfully, my brother was okay—wounded but okay. How could I allow my father to stay with me after all he'd done? Immediately I was involved in family drama, the same way I was when I lived there. I couldn't run nor hide from it. I eventually got my father to go and turn himself in, in Memphis, Tennessee, which he did. He was apprehended, and I went to court with my brother and mother, only to see my father in shackles standing before the judge being sentenced.

My mother separated from my father, and my family endured so much; we had to do a whole bunch of healing! My father later suffered a brain aneurysm, and a few strokes; he will never be the same. I practiced the *Green Light of Forgiveness* on my father, and today, I moved him and my mother from Memphis, Tennessee to live with me in Las Vegas, Nevada.

Some people might call me foolish (and they have), but the power of love overpowered hate and anger. *The Green Light of Forgiveness* allowed me to see my father from God's point of view, and I love him on a spiritual level. I do not love nor do I condone his evil acts; but I forgive him and by doing so, I see him through the lens with which God sees him. I don't make excuses for his behavior but I understand. My mother forgave him and she is still married to him, as she is his sole caregiver. My brother forgave him and my mother for staying with our repentant dad. Therefore, if the people who were directly affected by his psychosis could forgive him, as his daughter, I found it in my heart to forgive him as well.

Although we all forgave him, there are boundaries, which are strictly put into place. He has dementia and sometimes he can say mean things. When this happens, dementia or not, we do not allow any negative or hurtful talk from him, even if he isn't aware that he is doing it. He now emulates our spiritual calm and is pleasant for the most part. He has his space within our home, and I am being blessed for being able to forgive and move forward.

You do not have to live with the person who brought you pain, you do not have to be friendly with them at all. Do you remember my client Jessica who was sexually abused by her stepfather? Well, she has set boundaries into place where her own daughter is not allowed in his vicinity. If her mother wants to visit with her granddaughter, she must do so on Jessica's terms. This is perfectly understandable, and encouraged. You don't need any triggers or you should not be subjected to anyone who has brought you pain.

There are those of us who have reached enlightenment and have reached a level of forgiveness where we can forgive without hesitation. Again, it is all up to your level of comfort. Remember, set boundaries that are on your terms, and at your own level of comfort. You do not owe anyone anything.

Boundaries

Below is an example of boundary setting. These circles illustrate where you allow people to fall within your current boundaries.

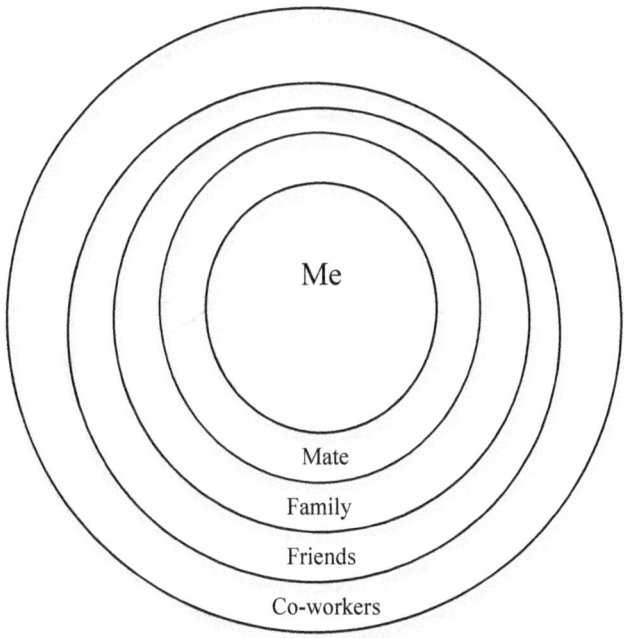

Take a piece of paper out and make a similar illustration of where you currently allow people to lie within your boundaries. Take note of your circles, do they overlap? Are they closer to your personal space than you'd like? Are some circles too large, which indicate your relationship with them is way out of reach? With your information, you can make changes as necessary.

Chapter

15
Release Shame & Guilt

"I release it all, I no longer hold on to the shame or guilt of the past."

You've done the work, you're aware of what trauma is, how it affects you, you've identified your triggers; you're getting your physical fitness on, eating right; you have sought out help, with chakras balanced and aligned, and you've even forgiven everything you can possibly think of. In essence, you feel ten pounds lighter, you're floating instead of walking, your friends are commenting on your new aura, and you're smiling from ear to ear. Now what?

Now it's time to ensure we don't slip back into our old patterns. Yes, we have made new patterns but in order to make sure we don't go back to our old way of thinking, with anger being at the center of it all, we have got to do some more work. Now, don't go cutting your eyes at me, or saying, "Toshia really? Girl please!" Yes, you've got more work to do. This is more self-work that most people ignore; so when situations rear their ugly heads and we start lowering our vibration to match those situations, we are falling into a couple of categories that can really take us there—shame and guilt.

Shame

"God looks at you adoringly, lovingly, He sees you as a magnificent creation with so much worth that He actually thought of you, and came up with every little thing about you and made it so."

 Although I did the work in my past and I made peace with my situations, I struggled with the leftover sediments of shame. Shame can make you hang your head without lifting your eyes to see your blessings. It can make you feel as if you aren't good enough to receive the blessings that the universe wants to gift you. If you don't remove shame from your energy field, it will have you living your life underneath a rock, afraid to peek out. For years, I hid away from my past life. I didn't tell anyone about what I'd been through for fear of what they might think of me or say about me, which is ridiculous because when God spares you, and delivers you from harm, or a less-than-stellar past, He doesn't think any less of you.

 Remember God is love, so if He loves us, why do we care what others think, say, or do? Well, I know this might be easier said than done. However, if we don't make peace with our past, the trauma that we've endured, it can continue to haunt us. It will continue to steer our decision-making, and wreck havoc on our thought patterns. I had this air about me, and it took away what I could get when it came to relationships because I felt and thought like, "Look at what I've been through, what man would want a woman who has been through something like I've been through? He's going to see me as damaged goods." But, what you have to know is that when God saves you, He makes you anew. I emerged a new woman, saved by His grace and mercy. I am not the old Toshia that went through so much low vibrational turmoil. The new Toshia is a woman of worth, a woman of value. I don't just bring stuff to the table, I made the table! So if you start to feel bad about what you've gone through, it means that you haven't truly forgiven yourself.

To overcome shame, you have to see yourself through the eyes of God. God looks at you adoringly, lovingly, He sees you as a magnificent creation with so much worth that He actually thought of you, and came up with every little thing about you and made it so. He knew what you were able to bring forth to this world before you took your first breath. So if someone treats you as if you ought to be ashamed of what you've gone through, it's time to set up boundaries, and get away from them. The question isn't if you're good enough, the question is, how could you not be? You are a magnificent creation in the eyes of God. You have to know this and hold your head up, look at people in the eye. If you aren't ready to speak your truth, then maybe you haven't cleared your throat chakra enough, and you haven't forgiven yourself the way God has. God has forgiven you, and He wants you to move forward with dignity and compassion.

Compassion is the gentleness, generosity, kindness, and love that you extend toward others. We very rarely include ourselves; but God wants us to start with ourselves first. Think about it for a moment, if you were to meet another person who has gone through what you have gone through in your past, how would you treat him or her? What would you say to this person to encourage him or her? What would you do for him or her to show them you care? Okay then, why not extend that same sort of compassion toward yourself?

If you are having a hard time having compassion toward self, then you are still struggling with your self-worth, and your third chakra is blocked, unbalanced, and in need of clearing. There is no difference between compassion toward self or others, so extend that same kind of love toward *you*. No one deserves your love and kindness more than you.

Guilt

"If you feel guilty, it is not of God, and you have to pull yourself up from that low vibrational place."

The effects of guilt can make you feel as if you have been going ten rounds in a boxing ring. Guilt leaves you worn out, tired, beat down, and dragging from self-defeat. If you have truly forgiven yourself, then you won't feel guilty about anything. Guilt stems from the notion that you should have done something, done more, stepped in, and saved someone or even yourself. It's the feeling that you haven't done enough to stop, prevent, or fix a certain situation. Let me tell you, nothing screams self-defeat more than guilt. It will eat you up internally, and you will suffer greatly especially in your solar-plexus, third chakra. When I suffered from guilt, I had horrible stomach ulcers and other problems. I cursed myself for not having better judgment. I didn't speak up for fear that someone would say, "Well, she deserved all that happened to her because she should have known better than to meet up with someone she barely even knew." I have clients that suffer from guilt, and state that although they know they were underage, they should have told someone that they were being victimized. Then there are the parents of children who have passed on that express guilt because their children are no longer alive—here in earthly form. If you suffer from guilt, you have not forgiven yourself, and peace will not find you.

My clients, who suffer from grief, can hardly sleep, or find peace within their lives. No matter what good they have found, guilt is somewhere lurking in the background, constantly reminding them that they don't deserve happiness because they didn't do enough, and they aren't good enough. God does not like guilt. He did not give you that. On the contrary, people think God places guilt in their lives, in their consciousness so that they can become aware whenever they do something wrong.

God is love, and He made you in His image. God doesn't suffer from guilt, and He doesn't want you to suffer from it either. Guilt, pain, suffering, and shame is not given to you from Him. He is only light, and the highest vibration. When you go to those depths, you have stepped down from the natural realm, in which He has placed you. You aren't supposed to feel that type of pain. If you feel guilty, it is not of God, and you have to pull yourself up from that low vibrational place. God is light, happiness, joy, peace, and love. You can't feel love and guilt at the same time. Therefore, you must choose; will you have self-love and love yourself the way God loves you, or will you be guilty, that which is not of God? If you feel guilt for anything, pray this prayer and repeat the Green Light of Meditation with you being the focus of forgiveness.

Once you have moved on from shame and guilt and you have accepted yourself the way God has accepted you, it's time to release it all. Take your deep five breaths, meditate, and repeat these affirmations to yourself, "I release it all, I no longer hold on to the shame or guilt of the past."

A prayer to help you release shame and guilt:

"God, help me to see myself as you see me. Help me to stop pointing fingers at myself, with feelings of inadequacy and guilt. Help me to see that I was made in your image, and that you have forgiven me, so that I will forgive myself. Help me to love myself the way you love me. Amen."

Chapter

16
Divine Connection

"The spiritual journey is the soul's life commingling with ordinary life. ~ Christina Baldwin"

Building a relationship with God is a very personal journey. It's not the type of adventure you can bring others in on. You see, you were created out of His love for you, and the one thing the Divine wants is a close relationship with you. I don't care what circumstances were surrounding your conception. You have purpose, and the Divine was the force behind that purpose. When you have a solid foundation with the Creator, you will find out this purpose, and will no longer question your existence. Also, when you have a personal connection, you will go to Him for everything! You will no longer rely on personal confidants to get sound advice. Sure, you will continue close relationships here on the earthly plane, but after building your relationship with the Creator, you will start to look inward. You and the Creator will enjoy close conversations through prayer, and meditation. I always like to say *with prayer, you are talking to God, and with meditation, you are listening.* You will long to get to know the Creator on a closer, more personal level once you start.

After the act of forgiveness, it takes trust. You have to trust God that He will see you through after you have practiced forgiveness, and you have to trust yourself. You may think you have to learn how to trust others again, but actually, you will have to learn how to trust yourself first.

Cynthia, a client who seemed to have the worst luck picking men was exhausted with dating. She stated that she seemed to be a bum magnet. She was discouraged because she felt that every man she chose was a liar, a cheat, and a loser. She felt she would never find the right mate. Cynthia thought she had a hard time trusting men, but actually, she had a hard time trusting herself. I had to tell Cynthia that it wasn't the men's fault, it was actually her low self-worth and low self-esteem that made her pick men who were of this caliber, and it was a cycle. I showed her that she didn't value herself enough, nor did she trust herself enough to pick someone who would be of a higher caliber. Cynthia admitted that although she believed in the Divine, she did not having a personal relationship with Him. This was most certainly evident in her choice of men. When you are connected with the Divine, you will choose someone who is a reflection of how you feel about yourself.

The years when I was involved with mentally and physically abusive men proved that I did not have a personal relationship with the Creator. This is evident because the Creator would never treat me the way I allowed those men to treat me. The Creator is pure love. The Creator looks at us adoringly and lovingly. The Divine fills your heart chakra with this positive and loving energy. When you look in the mirror, you see the Creator's reflection and you will treat yourself as such. Therefore, you would never allow anyone to mistreat you because the Creator does not mistreat you. Now of course, no one is perfect in their humanly actions.

In this same ideal, you would not mistreat yourself. If you looked at yourself adoringly and lovingly the way the Creator looks at you, you wouldn't dare misuse or abuse your body. No matter how flawed your physical body is, He chose that body for your spirit to reside. So it only seems right that you take care of the body the Creator gifted you with.

Jonathan drank heavily for ten years. In fact, when I met him, I was quite sure he was inebriated. When Jonathan's father passed away, he began to experiment with drugs and alcohol at the age of 17. He talked about how he would show up in class at school high, drunk, and he would sleep through his classes until he eventually stopped showing up altogether. He had multiple car accidents, near death experiences, and blackouts. We met while I was on my way to a speaking engagement; we sat next to one another on a plane. I asked Jonathan if he had a personal relationship with the Creator and he admitted that he did not. He stated that he stopped going to church with his mother while he was a child. I corrected him and stated that I wasn't talking about going to church, or practicing a sort of religion. I explained what I meant about having a personal relationship with the Creator. I also asked if he forgave himself for becoming an addict, dropping out of high school, and not loving himself enough to take care of himself better. He admitted that he had not. I then asked him if he had forgiven his father for passing away and leaving him at an early age. Again, he stated that he hadn't. We talked until our plan landed. Jonathan had not forgiven himself or his father. Therefore, his sobriety would be hard to keep up until he did so. I explained that he would always struggle with practicing self-love and respecting his body the way the Creator wanted him to until he practiced forgiveness, and saw himself through the eyes of the Creator.

It's important to note that we make mistakes, and we say things that we do not mean. We are spiritual beings having a spiritual experience. There is a difference in making a mistake and making the same mistake time and time again. When we continually repeat patterns that we regard as mistakes, they aren't mistakes at all; they become a decision. I chose to ignore the signs of abusive partners and made the decisions not only to become involved with them, but I also stayed. Here, we can rid ourselves of the victim mentality and accept that we made a conscious decision. When I did not have a personal relationship with the Creator, I allowed this mistreatment and could not see my value. When I formed a loving relationship with God, I stopped allowing this negative maltreatment and sought only loving and kind relationships with people who treated me as my Creator would. I have since forgiven my past mates for hurting me, set up boundaries, and, of course, I forgave myself for allowing the mistreatment to happen in the first place.

You will attract exactly what you feel you deserve. If you don't have a personal connection with the Divine to serve as your guide for how you should be treated, then you open yourself up to just about anything.

It is very easy to begin your relationship with the Divine. The very first thing you will need to do is say this prayer, which will open up the channel to begin your very personal and sacred journey:

> *"Creator, I humbly ask that you please forgive me for not allowing your sweet and holy voice to come through me. Divine teacher, I ask that you come to me and renew in me a clean heart, and open spirit. Beloved friend, I ask that you dwell within me, and walk alongside me while together we build our divine connection. And so it is"*

Divine Connection Meditation

Now that you have prayed this prayer, it is time to meditate to open your crown chakra to receive spiritual enlightenment. Do not eat anything heavy at least two hours prior to this meditation; do not take any drugs or alcohol. Ensure you are in a quiet space, and simply sit in a comfortable seated position with your legs crossed. Lay your hands on your knees with your palms up. You may close your eyes or open them. Take five deep breaths, breathing through your nose on the inhale, and blowing through your mouth on the exhale. When you have taken your breaths, say the following prayer in your mind:

Divine, I ask that you clear my crown chakra so that I can become open and spiritually connected with you in the way that you desire.

Now slow your thoughts by imagining a golden orb filling your head and gently growing and rising through the top of your head, toward the heavens. This soft golden light is elevating your thoughts of happiness and positivity. This golden light is now filing on the outside of your head, expanding as you become more open to the possibility of connecting with the heavens and the Divine in oneness. You are feeling this connection now journey from the top of your head toward your sixth chakra, it flows down softly towards your fifth chakra, it swirls toward your forth chakra and merges with the soft green light of the heart chakra. This color swirls and expands on the outside of your body, expands and engulfs your entire body. You sit with this light and feel lighter and connected with the Divine. You sit in bliss, knowing that you have journeyed inward; you are now connected with the Divine, and all is well.

A prayer to bless your new union with God:

"Dear God, I am thankful for being in your presence, for this new relationship that we have. I look forward to our new sacred journey together. Amen"

Chapter

17
Rebuild With Positive Thinking

Now that you have a new foundation on which you can build your new spiritual home, it's time to restructure your thinking. You see, keeping your thinking the same way as before will only be like dragging your old dilapidated furniture into an upscale, brand new penthouse. What's the point? Do you remember the television show, Beverly Hillbillies? Well, envision that for your current mindset. You can't move your old country ways into this upscale new body of yours. Honey, no! You're going to have to get used to a whole new way of thinking in order for it to work. I see this happening quite often with people; they come to me, learn new coping techniques and skills, but place them to the wayside because they settle back into their *comfortable* way of thinking and living. I call this negative mind chatter. I could write thirty more chapters, and coach you one on one, but if you keep your current mindset and neglect to practice forgiveness on every level, then it won't help you. Your mindset has to change, or your life will stay the same.

Miranda came to me desperate for change in her life. She stated that she had no idea what her life's purpose was, or how to go about finding out what it is. After our initial conversation and my assessment of her, I realized that she carried a lot of emotional baggage and resentment from childhood. She truly detested her twin sister. Miranda stated that her sister was the 'good twin,' her parents always compared them and so she ended up resentful about it. She spoke of her twin as if she were a stranger on the street, calling her Little Miss Perfect. There was no love in her voice, and I could visibly see pain in her eyes. She stated she knew it was wrong for her to feel this way but she couldn't help. She wished they weren't twins so she wouldn't be underneath so much pressure. I aligned Miranda's chakras with Reiki, and I helped her practice the Green Light of Forgiveness meditation. She needed to forgive herself for having these damaging thoughts of jealousy and incompetency; as well as forgive her parents for comparing her with her twin sister, and finally her sister for not standing up to their parents in her presence. She felt relieved but soon after, she reemerged at my office in need of additional help. What happened that she fell back into her old thinking patterns?

Miranda felt good about who she was as a person, she finally saw the value that she brought to the world, and looked forward to building her new online business, but she neglected to change her tape. Her new positive way of living and thinking fell apart when she joined her family for the holidays.

Miranda immediately allowed her self-worth and self-esteem to plummet the moment her sister arrived for dinner. Those old emotional wounds reopened, the negative tape started going again, and she allowed herself to shrink in size. I helped Miranda to see that it was no good for her to continue to make appointments with me if she wasn't going to remember and put into practice those things that I taught her. Really, some people may call me foolish for not taking money from her, but I think the total opposite. My goal is to help people move past trauma and pain toward something greater. I am not in the coaching business purely for money because, truth be told, if I keep people for too long, what does that say about my work? Right! I need people to pick themselves up, practice the tools and techniques that I teach them, and become self-sufficient.

Miranda stated she would definitely stop the damaging thought patterns of her past from preventing her from living her best life. We ended her session with a pact, which was the promise she made to herself to remember her value and purpose when faced with her past.

To change your tape, you have to use a portion of your brain to oversee the thought patterns that are emerging from your mind. This portion of the brain is like a security guard, in that it polices and protects all other aspects of the brain. It goes something like this:

Thought: "I look so fat in this dress today. I hate the way that I look."

Security part of the brain: "Not so fat, Missy! I will not allow this negative self-talk in the mind today! You look great; there is nothing wrong with the way you look. In fact, you look beautiful."

It's pretty easy, and I do it quite often, especially when I have to speak on stage in front of a new audience. I too have to secure my brain and ensure we are only allowing positive self-talk to form, as anything else is damaging and not serving me for my highest good.

Back to my client, Miranda, a couple of months later, I ran into Miranda at a community event, and she looked great. When I asked her what changed, she stated everything. In fact, she introduced me to her twin sister who was happily accompanying her at the event! As it turned out, she and her sister were spending more time together, and enjoying one another's company! I was thrilled. Miranda moved into her new spiritual space by changing her tape with new thoughts, forgiveness, and acceptance.

A prayer to avoid replaying the tape of negativity:

"Creator, I ask that you keep my mind clean and free from negativity. I ask that you change the tape indefinitely so that I can keep my mind on you, positive and free from negativity. Amen."

Now that you have done the work and you are on the pathway to forgiveness, write down what keeps coming up as negative mind chatter. Once you have it down and can see it in front of you, you can work on ways to combat it with positive thinking. An example has been provided for you

Negative Chatter	Positive Truths
You won't be forgiven for your mistakes!	God forgave me; therefore, I forgive myself.

Chapter

18
The Pact

"With your pact, the ego is not in the forefront; God is in the lead with His agenda. With God using His own agenda, He will use your skills, talent, and gifts. He will give you new ideas, dreams, and talents to pull it all together and make it happen."

I teach an e-course called, *The Pact*. The pact is all about assisting you in keeping the promises that you've made to yourself. At some point in your life, you made a vow to yourself. This promise held hope and forward progression. Now that you have forgiven yourself and others, or you are in the process of doing so, this is the perfect time to revisit or make a pledge to yourself if you have never made one.

Sometimes, we make a pact with God and ourselves out of fear or suffering. For instance, while I was going through my trauma, I promised God that if He saved me, I would help and save others. I made this promise out of my last ditch effort to get out of a dire situation. People make these pacts with God all of the time. How about the man who promised God that if He saved his wife, who was dying from breast cancer, he would be the best husband in the world? These are all desperate pacts that we make out of fear and suffering.

Will God hold you to these pacts if He so calls, *saves you?* You betcha! I should know because you are reading this book right now, which is the product of the pact I made with God. Did I really plan on helping others and saving other people once I became saved from trafficking, honestly no. I mean, I just wanted to live my life without drama, pain, and trauma. Will the man whose wife made a miraculous improvement really become the best husband on earth? I guarantee he didn't. No one is perfect; the man was just desperate and had nowhere else to go, or no one else to turn to. We can even get more relatable, and I'll ask you when was the last time you promised God something only to really get something in return? Consider, for instance, the following:

- God, if you let me get out of this traffic ticket, I will never speed again.
- If you allow this plane to arrive safely, I promise I'll go to church every Sunday from now on!
- God, if you spare me this one time and let my test come back clean, I'll never sleep with someone without protection again, I swear!

Yes, I went there, because someone reading this book right now has made that very promise! The Creator knows we have no intention in keeping these promises and sometimes He lets us get by with these pacts, and other times, well, you're reading this book, aren't you?

I knew the Creator wanted to collect on my promise of helping others, so I volunteered at domestic violence shelters in Atlanta, Georgia, and in Memphis, Tennessee. Still I knew it wasn't enough, I had to do more. I needed to honor God in other ways so my non-profit, Purple W.I.N.G.S. was born, and I truly felt as if I were fulfilling my pact. God was thoroughly pleased with my philanthropy but I still felt the tug in my heart to do more, give more. When was enough going to be enough? While meditating, the answer came to me loud and clear. God wanted me to work for Him personally—not only through my non-profit, but also He wanted to use me entirely. I was doing His will but I was neglecting my true inner calling. My inner calling wanted me to surrender, and allow my gifts to be used exclusively by Him, to bring forth love and healing throughout the world. That is what this book is about, healing through love and forgiveness. I was so anxious to keep the pact of success for myself, to be a great speaker and a transformational life coach that I buried God's message and put my own will in the forefront. I was being led by my ego. With your pact, the ego is not in the forefront; God is in the lead with His agenda. With God using His own agenda, He will use your skills, talent, and gifts. He will give you new ideas, dreams, and talents to pull it all together and make it happen.

Your pact can be about obtaining success and having money. Money is good, and a great tool. Money is energy. If your energy is on a high vibration, then you will attract money and all things that are for your highest good, with God being at the center of it all. Your promise has to be in line with God, and then success will be inevitable. Success will be in the form of peace, with the foundation of love. I have mentored successful people whose core was their ego. They were miserable too in other areas of their lives. There was never an even playing field. They had the money, expensive annual vacations, and beautiful material possessions but the inner peace was absent, and there was no divine connection. Without a foundation on which to stand, everything else is temporal and lacking. Without a firm foundation, your success is temporal, and it will surely fall. This is one reason some people can be extremely poor, but have a divine connection and be one of the *richest* people in the world. You must have a spiritual foundation, a divine connection with the Creator at the core.

You have forgiven yourself and others; it's time to remember or make a unique promise to yourself to have something to aspire you and to work for. It's time to use your unique talents and gifts for your highest good. It's time to reach your unique potential by honoring that promise and keeping the Divine at the center of it all. What is your pact and how will you honor it? Go to the greenlightofforgiveness.com and find some unique ways in which to discover your pact, or create one.

Here is a prayer to ask God for guidance with your pact:

"Dear God, I ask that you help me rediscover the pact that I made with myself and restructure it to include you. I ask that you help me to keep true to myself with you being at the core. I ask that you take the lead and help me use my gifts for my highest good. I ask that you help me to continue to remain positive, uplifted, and encouraged. I ask that you help me to forgive as you do, with agape love being at the center of it all. Amen"

The Pact

Use the area below to either rediscover your pact, or formulate one!

Meaningful past events that shape who I am as a person:

_____
_____
_____
_____
_____

These meaningful events help me to become:

_____
_____
_____

Who are you?

_____
_____

What skills, talents, and gifts do you have to offer?

_____
_____

What will your pact be?

_____

Conclusion

You have read this book, and completed the exercises; and it has given you a guide and some tools, to heal your trauma, practice forgiveness, and go forward with your new life. You have done the hard work, which is actually forgiving yourself first and others who have hurt you. If you continue to practice forgiveness, you will see a huge shift. You will feel lighter, happier, and at peace. If you accept your history, honor it, and respect it, you will be able to move past it and live a peaceful life. You will also be able to help others who may have or currently be suffering. It is only when we do the hard work, and realize our pact will we be able to help others. This is all God truly wants for us, to heal, and to help others. Love is at the core of it all. To see this, we must be willing to be a servant of peace for the Creator.

It has been my complete joy to be used as God's vessel to talk about the art of forgiving. If I can be of help in other ways, to bring you even more healing, please visit and contact me at toshiashaw.com.

In Love & Light,

Toshia
SHAW

About the Author

Toshia Shaw is a Human Services professional who specializes in behavioral health, holistic mental health, and energy healing. She mentors women who suffer from the effects of drug addiction, sexual assault, sex-trafficking, domestic violence, grief, loss, and other traumatic experiences, which shape the way they view themselves and the world around them. She is the Founder and Executive Director of Purple W.I.N.G.S. (PWs), a 501 c (3) non-profit girls mentoring organization; and Toshia Shaw, The Professional Mentor, LLC., a trauma-informed, life coaching agency, and energy healing company.

She is an accomplished, motivational speaker for the Jodi Solomon Speakers Bureau. As a life coach, she helps women who have experienced traumatic events in their lives to overcome their past traumas and transform their lives. Through group mentoring, e-courses, and one-on-one coaching, Toshia helps others to cultivate a new way of living that will enable them to attract the kind of relationships, success, and happiness that they truly deserve.

Toshia is a certified Reiki Master, and intuitive healer combining spirituality and intuition, with the use of the five senses to locate and correct imbalances in the energy flow within the body. She does this by touch and long distance healing where she focuses on physical, emotional, and sexual wellness.

To get in touch with Toshia, simply visit her website, *www.ToshiaShaw.com.*

References

* "dōTERRA is a trademark of dōTERRA International, LLC, all rights reserved."
* "SARA is a trademark of Young Living Essential Oils, all rights reserved."
* Smith, M., and Robinson, Lawrence, M.A., and Segal, J. PhD., (2016). "PTSD: Symptoms, Self-Help, Coping Tips and Treatment." Retrieved on January 15, 2016 from http://www.helpguide.org/articles/ptsd-trauma/post-traumatic-stress-disorder.htm.
* Massachusetts General Hospital (2012, November 12). Meditation appears to produce enduring changes in emotional processing in the brain. Science Daily. Retrieved January 4, 2016 from http://www.sciencedaily.com/releases/2012/11/121112150339.htm
* Numbers 16:30-34; King James Bible.
* Got Questions ministry, retrieved on November 13, 2015 from www.gotquestions.org.
* Shapiro, F. (2001). "Trauma Recovery, EMDR Humanitarian Assistance Programs." Retrieved on December 8, 2015 from http://www.emdrhap.org/content/what-is-emdr/
* Jacobson, E. (1938). Progressive Relaxation. Chicago: University of Chicago Press.
* Chakras Icons Photo © Peterhermesfurian | Dreamstime.com - http://www.dreamstime.com/royalty-free-stock-photo-chakras-icons-image37767185#res11237428
* Shapiro, F. (2001). "Eye movement desensitization and reprocessing: Basic principles, protocols, and procedures (2nd ed.)." New York: Guilford Press.

www.ingramcontent.com/pod-product-compliance
Lightning Source LLC
Chambersburg PA
CBHW031549040426
42452CB00006B/254